To: Ada

MEMOIRS
OF A BRIDE WHO WAITED

Based on a true story

Helping women find hope, healing and
wholeness in the detours of life while in
the pursuit of true love.

DOLCIEBELLA ELLIOTT

WOW Book Publishing™

With Love,
Dolciebella

CONTENTS

TESTIMONIALS

Dolciebella is very passionate about both God and people. She is one of the most selfless people I have come across, she is a great giver who empowers people without holding back. She is very caring, and always wants people to succeed. She is a great communicator who is eloquent and versatile. A personal friend with great ethics. I highly recommend this book, read it and be empowered. It's hard to meet the author and not be.

—*Rev Felix Appiah*
Elim Rehoboth
London, UK

As a teenager, I worked as a cleaner in a hotel and in a chance meeting, I met Dolciebella when I turned up to clean her room. She was in Ghana to adopt an orphan. I happened to be an orphan and was simply finding my daily bread. She spoke with me compassionately an adopted me into her heart, encouraged me to go to school, got me a car so I can be an Uber driver and rented me a place to live. She encouraged me to study and make something of my life—always telling me no one will take my education from me. I can never repay her. I have been to many occasions and heard her speak. She is compassionate, articulate and very funny. She wrote this book mainly for women, but as a man, I have been blessed by it.

—*Kingsley Kumi*
Student and Adopted son
Ghana.

Dolciebella is a blessing to know. She is very inspiring and has impacted not only my life but countless of other people's lives as well. She is truly a woman of God who lets God use her as His arms extended to those she meets. Among other things, she is an amazing writer and a great empathetic communicator. This book will bless people in whatever season of life they are. Great tools and tips.

—*Daba Wedemeyer*
Nurse
Germany

Dolciebella is a generous human being, an excellent business woman, a loving mother, a caring daughter, a supportive sister, a good aunt, an awesome friend and above all, a great author. Through her writing she carries and transforms her readers through her illustrations. This book comes highly recommended. Simple, relatable and transformative is what it is.

—*Melvin and Mercy D'Cunha*
Border Force Officer and Accountant
London, UK

Dolciebella is my lifelong friend and confidant. I have always admired her drive, determination, ambition, wit and compassion. Her passion for her humanitarian work with the underprivileged is a testament to her selflessness. As an author she is very articulate and this book effectively communicates its essence to the readers.

—Victor Harding
PSO Officer
Maryland, USA

Dolciebella has been a friend to me for over 35 years—a testament to her loyalty. She has grown from my wonderful, vivacious, fun-loving comrade in mischief, to my steadfast life-long friend and confidante. She has always been good with words and has a natural gift for turning everyday events into funny captivating narratives. The genre she has chosen as the launch pad for this new season of life, is therefore no surprise. What a joy to have my friend use her gifting to positively impact women with this legacy!

—Elaine Anderson
Medical Doctor
Liverpool, UK

If I should describe Dolciebella, I would use the colour green. Her energy springs new green shoots of life in all her undertakings. She is fresh in her approach to life and creates room for endless possibilities. She takes her readers to that place of liberation.

—Usifu Jalloh
Story teller
London, UK

Having known Dolciebella for over 26 years, she is one of the kindest, most loving, selfless and caring people I have ever met. Although she is ambitious, professional and outgoing, she is humble and down to earth and that makes her an amazing person. She has a heart for people and have always championed the cause of those in adversity to give them a better story. This book is a testament of that passion. Furthermore it is a practical tool in the hands of those who are serious about transformation and wholeness.

—*Sydney Martindale*
Programme Manager
London, UK.

Dolciebella is an amazing person who has a gift of encouragement. She is a very intelligent, hardworking and compassionate author who writes with conviction.

—*Romerlyn Joseph*
Musician
London, UK

Dolciebella is a very caring and committed human being. She always keeps in mind the well-being of those she loves. I have always admired her generosity and kindness. In addition to being very intelligent, she is very creative, highly organised and strategic. With her transparency you will always know her true feelings. As an author, her communication skills are outstanding. She expresses her thoughts and feelings in simple and deep ways that appeal to a vast audience. Her

FOREWORD

Dear Reader,

Memoirs of a Bride who Waited is a book that is timely with nuggets that will help women in all walks of life. Dolciebella has gained a lot of life experiences that she uses to channel her passion for helping others through the way she captures and tells this true-life story.

This book is relatable, practical, inspiring, and relevant for those who need to understand how to navigate the emotional waters that they may find themselves in as they open their hearts to encounter true love.

Dolciebella carries her readers on an amazing journey and they will be left knowing they can have emotional well-being in a world where stereotypes define relationship expectations and the conflict it often poses against personal core values.

This book is definitely a gem in the treasure box of any library.

—Vishal Morjaria
Award Winning Author, *Master your WOW*
Transformational International Speaker

ACKNOWLEDGEMENTS

I acknowledge God; Our Father—My Father; who makes all things possible. He who has strengthened and supported me through the tough times. There was a time when I couldn't see the wood for the trees, but through his mighty hand, I have been endowed with the gift of empowering others. By grace, He has made this work possible.

I acknowledge and appreciate my parents, who although they were not perfect, loved and raised me as best they could; I thank them for guiding me the best way they knew how. They taught me to pursue my dreams and to know that no matter what life throws at me, I have to keep reaching for the finish line. To my brothers, you guys rock. You gave me so many fun life experiences. Thanks for always having my back.

I acknowledge my son. My little (now 6 feet tall) munchkin, you are my inspiration never ending. You give me a reason to keep going when the corridors of life get dark. I love you, bless you and give you as a gift to the world. Let your light shine unapologetically.

I acknowledge, salute, and celebrate all the people who have contributed in various ways to making me who I am today. You are way too many to name. I love and appreciate you all.

To 'my children' in the various orphanages and all those who have allowed me to be a blessing in fulfilling my life's ambitions, thank you.

To Avril, thank you for allowing me to tell your story.

Finally, to you my readers, I acknowledge you for receiving this book and letting it inspire you.

When stories are told, it enables, equips, and empowers others to know that they are not alone. It provides them room to tell their own stories, too. I hope this book a blessing to you.

AVRIL'S STORY

Hailing from Freetown, Sierra Leone, a small country in West Africa and with the blood of repatriated freed slaves running through her veins, Avril, is the only girl of four children. Her mother says she was an 'easy' baby. Making her entrance into the world weighing only 6 lbs. She proved to be a contented baby who developed very quickly—walking and talking by the age of 9 months. She is rather easy-going, although very decisive and a very clear thinker. Avril grew up to be a mother by choice, an IT consultant by profession, and an advocate for the next generation to maximize their currency of life—time! She possesses a keen sense of purpose, which enables her to live a goal-oriented life.

By virtue of her experience as a child in a stable, loving family, she grew up desiring to have a marriage that mirrored and even bettered that of her parent's own—which in itself was a fairy-tale unfolding before her eyes. She longed for a knight in shining armour to rescue her like a damsel in distress, but her journey to the realisation of that fairy tale was a hell of a rollercoaster ride. Through the experiences and insights of her childhood, she grew to love the finer things of life and despised lack and insufficiency, mediocrity, and anything that is not done with excellence. She worked hard, and God blessed her efforts.

Even though she could not draw a stickman, she carries a keen appreciation for the arts with an insatiable love for museums, art galleries, music in general, particularly jazz and classical music, especially the Philharmonic Orchestra. She loves to cook and loves good food. As she fondly says: "there are some things you can't eat with your shoes on. You need to take off your shoes, so you can wiggle your toes." She is a deeply romantic soul who loves flowers, candles, and perfumes with an expressive gift of words and a kind touch. She is well travelled, loves to explore how other cultures live and what drives their survival. She is intrigued by the diversity of life.

She does not suffer fools gladly, and although she is a strong-willed, dynamic, go-getter who is deemed a high achiever by many, she has a soft, tender, spontaneous and very loving streak that makes her vulnerable at the best of times.

Avril's life is enriched by healthy interpersonal and blood relationships. She walks into a room and lights it up with her smile. She is confident, driven, well-presented, academically astute, and strikingly beautiful; however, her journey to the altar—the deepest desire of her heart—meeting her prince and being taken in marriage has been a journey worth sharing.

On the terrace in of a period villa in Frascati, an elevated town on the outskirts of Rome, Avril sits, sipping hot chocolate as she overlooks the city of Rome on a beautiful warm evening as the sun sets. Suddenly, it dawns on her that the journey she embarked on, fuelled by fantasies and daydreams, the journey to find that prince, that knight in shining armour, led her straight to her own heart where she discovered hidden riches in secret places. She sighs. It all makes sense. Suddenly, life makes sense. The dark clouds, the disappointments, the failed relationships in the now perfect picture of her life, makes sense. She found herself.

She feels beautiful, like a flower in full bloom. She has tapped into a mystery that few on this side of eternity understand or fully experience. She suddenly puts the pieces together and understands that life is not a sprint but a marathon. It is not how fast you run but how well you run that determines the quality of the race. She looks back at the journey so far and even though she has loved and lost, suffered betrayal, unemployment, homelessness, and imprisonment—all in the name of love—her life now blossoms because she found herself.

Her Prince Charming is well worth the wait—and now she waits patiently and with great peace. She recognises that the value of her worth is priceless. She is like coal that has gone through the passage of time and pressure to now shine like the diamond she always was. The journey has had thorns and thistles, delays and distractions, disappointments and disillusionments, yet by some supernatural unexplained means, she has managed to keep her eyes on the finish line and kept running. Now, her heart is beautiful, she exhales, takes another sip, realising how lovely and rich the cup of hot chocolate she is having, actually is, looks up into the sky, and whispers, "God, you were there all along, I have found myself! I am whole!"

This is her story . . .

BLUE SKIES

*C**lick, clack, click, clack.*

The sound of Avril's heels against the pavement as she walks briskly along with her bag in one hand and her iPad in the other. It's a cold, wet, miserable day, even though it's meant to be spring!

"Typical British weather!" She exclaims on the phone to Rosa, who is lounging at this moment in the warmth and comfort of her home. Far be it for Rosa to swap her warmth for the cold and wet. She loves a comfy life.

"It's miserable out here", she shares. "On a day like this, I really wish I had a nice man waiting for me at home, so I can go cuddle up." There is a longer than expected silence down the phone line.

"Avril, I've told you are the only woman I know who says the things you say."

Avril responded, "Rosa, you really need to go out more! You are too conservative, quiet, and cagey about your needs. What's wrong with a girl desiring some biceps or triceps to embrace her on a day like this?"

"Avril, you know, all my life I have never quite met someone like you. You are like a man. Straight talking, and I bet you take no prisoners. Imagine you giving 'it' a name.

Trust me girl, don't think I will ever take anyone called Molly seriously ever again!" Rosa laughs and rearranges herself on her sofa. "Where are you?"

"I'm on my lunch break, walking towards the office building next door to get something to eat," Avril replies.

Avril was walking slightly uphill and beginning to feel a bit sore. In fact, with each forward movement of her legs, her thighs and her butt cheeks hurt. She had been exercising and may have overdone it a bit. She was just beginning to drift off into a daydream about the man of her dreams giving her a well-deserved massage when the sound of Rosa's voice interrupted her thoughts. "How are things at work?"

"Things are good. I can't complain." She replied slowly with a slight stutter. Avril paused briefly as she chose a hot meal that looked tantalising. Rosa, patient as ever, waited on the other end of the phone line. "Okay. I am nicely settled down to devour my plate of cannelloni and obligatory veg after having cast my eyes all around this restaurant just in case there's any talent. Guess what? There isn't! Same ole, same ole." She said, "Anyway, guess who called?"

"Akin? Again? What does he want this time?" Rosa asked with some irritation in her voice.

"Girl, I think he reckons I am mad. Well, I must have been mad to have gone out with him in the first place. He said he is sorry, wants one more chance to prove his love. He reckons he must have been possessed by the devil to have cheated on me. He went on with a long explanation of how much he misses me and how desperately he wishes he could turn the clock back. Of course, I told him where to go. Girl, I need to raise my game in judging people before I plunge into their world. I am such a poor judge of character. Right now, though, I need to devour this delicious delight and get back to converting my time into Pound Sterling. So how do you fancy us doing a week in Portugal for my birthday? I fancy some sun on my skin. Seriously, I need some vitamin D."

"Are you kidding me? Choose the date girl, and I am all yours." Rosa replied.

Portugal

Rosa and Avril booked a week in the sun and jetted off to make the most of a week's guaranteed warmth. They spared no expense. They booked an all-expenses paid, 5-star spa resort in Albufeira, within walking distance of the beach and a bus ride to the town centre. Their first impressions of Portugal: Landscape, check!—Lovely, with very scenic, views. Locals, check!—People seemed warm and friendly. Location, check!—Streets impeccably clean and gardens well kept. The suite in the hotel was simply amazing—double check. When they disembarked from the airport shuttle and walked into the lobby of the hotel, they could hardly contain their excitement. It is very classy, upscale and absolutely breath-taking.

The atrium seemed to be as high as the sky, and the marble floors glisten like they are sprinkled with fragments of diamonds. They were escorted to their suite, and squealed in delight when the doors glided open.

"Oh, my days! Girl, in all my travels never have I ever been in such a beautiful place! Look at the Mediterranean Sea. Oh, my world. We are going to be waking up to this view every day!"

The room was like an apartment. It was a proper suite

and beautifully coordinated with a colour scheme that was very calming. It had lush furnishings, majestic wardrobes, and a delightful view of the sea from a private balcony. They jumped on the beds like 5-year olds, occasionally giving each other high-fives.

"This is the life," Rosa says.

"This is the life indeed," Avril agrees. "It's going to be so hard going back to the UK after this." They both resolve with dogged determination to have a blast.

"No sad moments! Pinky swear?" Rosa says as she reached out her little finger. Avril reached out and locked her pinky in. It's a done deal. This is going to be an amazing break.

They ate and drank, chilled and shopped and had a really great, girlie bonding time. However, most of the time their discussions were focused on the lack of good quality men in their generation and also the poor quality of relationships around them. While in Portugal, they played a game they invented on the plane called 'Tasty Local Talent.' Basically, if either of them spotted an eligible-looking bachelor, they would earn 5 points, totalling their scores at the end of each day. Day after day, it was a tie with neither of them scoring anything. This triggered several conversations late into the night about whether their standards were too high and therefore, unattainable, whether they were too picky or whether in fact they live in times where good calibre men are just simply hard to come by.

They both resolved they would obviously love to get married and vocalised their daydreams about what their individual lives would look like with their significant others. They discussed what they are looking for in potential mates and pacified each other that surely 'The One' must be out there.

They spent some time during the week going into the local shops and gazing admiringly at all the little knick knacks arranged on the shelves. Portugal is adorable, and the shops all have such nice, cute little gifts. They went from store to store, "oohing" and "aahing."

Just as they were about to leave one of the shops, Rosa pointed to a rather interesting little item in a basket; it was a carving of a man's penis—and a large one at that. They stopped dead in their tracks, falling over each other, giggling uncontrollably. The shop assistant innocently walks up to them and asks if she could help. Still unable to speak from the fits of laughter, they childishly point to the carving. The lady at the checkout leans over and shouts, "Nice souvenir, you must buy!"

Avril looks up and asks, "Are the Portuguese men circumcised?" Gesticulating to get the question fully understood.

"Ah, yes! We chop the boy's young," she replies with a big grin and a naughty glint in her eye.

This response tickled them all the more. They ran out of the shop laughing. When they caught their breath, Avril stood and grabbed Rosa's shoulders. "Girl, I have decided to seriously add Portuguese men to my list. You mean they get the chop? Girl, we are on to something. High five!"

Rosa shook her head and rolled her eyes with a 'there-you-go-again' head nod. The rest of their holiday went on uneventfully, both Rosa and Avril learned new things about each other and their friendship certainly deepened. They returned to England and hit the ground running with their individual lives, but without doubt, more refreshed and rejuvenated from the trip.

A few months after they returned, it was Rosa's birthday. Avril and a couple of Rosa's married friends decided to meet up for a meal. They went to the famous Blue Water Shopping Centre—the biggest shopping centre in Europe and chose a nice restaurant. Avril baked a lovely Victoria sponge cake, and they had a very delightful meal with the cake as dessert. As is typical when women get together, the conversations quickly descended into the antics of men and the essence of their existence on the planet. It was interesting to Avril that the married ladies in the group weren't raving about being married at all. To her, it seemed like people were simply going through the motions and just resolved to live the life they found themselves in, especially, if children were in the mix. This left her thinking a lot about her own life and whether she was actually missing out a lot on what she thought marriage should look and feel like.

Later in the year, she made two trips to the U.S. in quick succession: one for business and the other for pleasure. Her business trip was intense and short. She flew back again a few weeks later and took time to smell the flowers and opted to spend time with some of her relatives. She was warmly welcomed to stay with one of her cousins, Rod and his wife. Being the tease that she is, she asked her cousin-in-law when their wedding anniversary was, as she wanted to "bless" her with something nice but naughty. Co-incidentally, it wasn't that far off, so Avril got her ants to work and decided on a treat from Victoria's Secret. On the day before they were scheduled to go, Avril was chilling with a book in her room when her cousin-in-law stealthily came into the room. She took a glace down the hallway and gently closed the door. Avril was taken aback by her sneaky movements but held her tongue patiently so she could fully understand what was really happening. "I think your cousin, my darling husband, has left. Phew! I need to talk to you so badly," she whispered.

"What's the matter love? Are you okay? Is everything okay?" Avril asked inquisitively.

"I just need you to hear me out. We never get time alone, and I really need to talk," she continued in a whisper. "Things are not good. Our marriage is in a lot of jeopardy. I just don't know what to do. He doesn't make love to me. In fact, he hardly ever does. We have been married for 4 years, and we have only had 3 intimate encounters. I really don't think he finds me attractive. I am hurting at a level that is hard to put into words. If he doesn't want me now when I am young and have good looks, is it when I am an old woman with wrinkles and grey hair that he'll want me? He doesn't want us to have kids. He says he has no money to raise children. Avril, what do I do? I cook him gourmet meals. I cook and clean and do what I can to seduce him. Where have I missed it?" Then, she started crying uncontrollably. She was absolutely inconsolable. Avril held her as she sobbed.

Avril's heart sank! Wow! She thought. Hmmm! This thing called marriage uh!

When she stopped crying, they spoke about things. Avril urged her to seek counselling; although, clearly, things looked very bleak. "I can't!" she said. She was convinced Rod will consider it a betrayal of trust. So she graciously opted to pass on the gift. She felt there was no reason for her to try to plan a steamy wedding anniversary.

It turned out he had told her on numerous occasions,

"Girl, there must be something wrong with you, cause I really just can't make love to you." To say Avril was dumbfounded by these revelations was an understatement. In her company, they seemed totally inseparable and in love. The whole marriage was a lie and their public display of affection was simply for the eye seeing of men. For the rest of her stay, Avril carefully observed and wondered how many other couples are living the same lie.

On the plane heading back for the UK, Avril's mind was flooded with confusion, trying to make sense of the revelations she had just had in the conversations with her in-law.

She followed up with her a few weeks after she returned, only to find that she had resolved to living the lie. "I have nowhere to go Avril. Maybe one day things might change. In the meantime, I am going to continue being a dutiful wife and hope for the best."

Avril resolved not to get involved. After digesting the whole matter, she was infuriated. Had she gotten involved, it would have resulted in the breakup of their marriage.

At this point, she had been divorced and was open to a new relationship. She felt that life had taught her some tough, emotional lessons and dealt her some difficult cards, yet by the things she had been exposed to over the years, she was moving to a place of gratitude for her life and questioning whether indeed she had been missing out. That evening when she went to bed, she let her mind wander and came into a realisation that actually, a lot of people are actually living a lie!

She recollected a few years back when a close friend of hers had gone through a divorce and executed her 'revenge' on men by sleeping around indiscriminately. Finally, she met and fell in love with a really great guy. In Avril's eyes, their relationship was near perfect. They seemed to have great chemistry, open communication, and a really strong bond. However, when the opportunity arose, the guy in question would flirt with other women openly. At one point, he even began to pursue Avril while he was still very much in a relationship with her friend.

His actions were dismissed as 'playful' and 'flirtatious' by his girlfriend, Avril's friend. She at that point had decided that no matter what this guy threw at her, this was it. She was in love and wasn't going to lose her man, especially as she was overweight and had concluded that she might not find someone else to be with. Disrespectfully, the guy would declare his feelings for other women in her face, yet her resolve to stay with him was unshaken.

In another experience, Avril's family threw her a surprise birthday party and hired a well-known friend of the family to photograph the occasion. This guy did not only have a photography and videography business, he was an accomplished musician who, at the time, presented a 20-year marriage with a beautiful wife to the world. When they met to review the proofs of the pictures he had taken, the guy began to heavily discredit his wife, rendered his marriage of no value and began to pursue Avril, convincing her he would leave his 'incapable' wife in a heartbeat. There were numerous other married men who had chased her, claiming their marriages were just a piece of paper. It never ceased to amaze her why men were generally so non-committal.

On discovering that women too, knew their marriages were in shambles and that many stayed not for love but out of feeling trapped or for the sake of kids or the backlash of public opinion, Avril realised she had a lot going for her. She became even more determined not to settle for anyone less than who she desired as God's best for her life. These realisations, however, left her with more questions than answers. She honestly begins to wonder what marriage is all about. Has she created this utopia that doesn't really exist?

She took a look at her life. She only saw blue skies. Her relationship with God is intact. She is out of debt and is emotionally stable. She isn't in a relationship, but she has recovered well from a divorce. She is doing fine, in fact, much more emotionally stable than a lot of people. She is well and in reasonably good health. She resolved that there is no point in selling herself short and settling for someone who will not add value to her life and improve her quality of life. She began to understand what she needs from a man rather than what she wants. Subconsciously, her paradigms were being formed, and her life experiences have a lot to do with that.

A while had elapsed and she had not seen Rosa, so she invited her and Janet, another friend she had known since primary school, over for a meal.

It is a lovely, crisp spring day. Avril spent most of it shopping and cooking as she prepared for her dinner party. She decided it was going to be a Mediterranean evening, so she prepared warm chicken salad with pesto, sundried tomatoes, olives, and avocado for starters. For mains, there were grilled lamb chops, spiced jewel rice with pine nuts, dressed with fresh parsley, and Sicilian lemon cheesecake for dessert. She meticulously prepared the food and made some ginger-spiced homemade lemonade to wash it all down.

Janet and Rosa, as they had done on many occasions, arrived and made themselves at home. As they prepared to dine, Janet remarked what a domestic goddess Avril is. "You are such a great cook!"

"It's my passion. The kitchen is my favourite place" Avril responded. "Magic happens here! Had I not pursued an academic path in life, I would definitely have ended up as another Gordon Ramsey, I am sure. I love that I can go into my kitchen and feel like a magician, whipping up edible things from raw ingredients. My kitchen is my office—my theatre. It's where I express my feelings in a way that is hard to describe. Baby girl, damn! I love to cook!" They continue chatting, talking about all things food, culture, weather, and of course, men.

They settled down to eat, and both Janet and Rosa remarked how much Avril seemed settled emotionally. She definitely had an aura of serenity about her, an inner confidence and joy that seems to spring up from deep within.

She told them that she has finally found herself. She remarked that in the last few months, she has felt like a flower in full bloom. "I suddenly understand the expression 'In the prime of life.'" She said as she gave them a twirl. "I feel beautiful from inside, and this has nothing to do with the validation of men. I am a masterpiece in the hand of God. He is moulding me and shaping me. The pieces of my life juxtapose perfectly, and I suddenly see clearly. And more importantly, I understand. I understand my journey so much better. I am thankful even for my moments of pain and lessons of past failures. I have come face-to-face with my fears and insecurities. I have now understood that in the times when I look back and see only one set of footprints, God was carrying me.

I have battled and overcome the demons of rejection and abandonment. In the end, I win. We all win if only we understand wholeness. I have learnt how to navigate cultural minefields and be productive. Life has taught me that the best me I could be is the authentic me, the real me, the me God meant for me to be since I was a clot of blood in my mother's womb. I have resolved to live unapologetically and to be true to myself. My worth does not depend on the opinions of others, the pressures of society, or the expectations of my cultural biases. My humanity is solidified. I am a citizen of the universe, and I have a right to not only be here but to also dent the sands of time with my presence. This smile you see, is fuelled from a heart of gratitude for the gift of life. I am going to make mine count."

There was ghostly silence as Janet and Rosa digested what Avril has just said. "My, my, my Avril, you have stumbled on some truths girl. I like your vibe. That confidence, girl, is going to take you places and open doors." Rosa said.

"Well my disposition has come from purpose being birthed from pain. Let me give you girls my story. Most of it you know, but hopefully if you survive this marathon, you will understand things from my perspective, and it might bring some illumination if it resonates with seasons on your journeys too." Avril said as she cleared the table.

They move into the living room with the leftover chilled jug of lemonade and make themselves very comfortable as they knew it was going to be a long night. They listen keenly as Avril shared her heart . . . .

CHILDHOOD MEMORIES

I walked onto the back porch and looked into the starlit sky. It must have been about 10pm, and at almost age 10, it was well past my bed time. There was a light breeze, and the night was dry and warm. As I sat on the steps leading into the yard, I looked up and for the first time questioned the existence of God. "God, who are you? Where are you anyway? Are you really there? Are you really invisible or do you just not like your clothes?" I ask as I gazed upwards at the sky.

"If you are, prove yourself to me!" Little did I know that this conversation with God will echo through the corridors of time in the decades to come as I came to experience this thing called life. *There must be God somewhere*, I thought as my mum called out for me, not believing I was not in my bed. I hastily retired to bed. As I rolled off to sleep, I thought, *all those stars couldn't have just been sprinkled in the sky by some unexplained means.*

Being the only girl of four kids, I felt quite special. I felt deeply loved, especially by my dad, and I was treated well by my brothers—well, for the most part. My father, a descendant of freed slaves who found themselves in Nova Scotia, Canada, had very good looks, a gentle demeanour, and a love for life.

Apart from being dashingly handsome, he was kind, gentle, of a quiet spirit, and extremely hardworking. He set the precedence of how I expected men to treat me and what an eligible bachelor should bring to the table. He was a good and demonstrable lover to my mum whose parentage hails maternally from Trinidad and paternally from Nigeria. By a sequence of events too convoluted to delve into, my parents met and married in Sierra Leone.

My mum, tall, dark, curvaceous, and beautiful was the disciplinarian, and her disciplinary measures, which only made sense to me as an adult, deterred me from being bonded to her at a young age. It seemed I could get away with murder where my dad was concerned, but mum seemed to have eyes in the back of her head. Nothing seemed to escape her attention. Being an excellent cook, I found myself aspiring to cook like her as I have always loved good food and would spend hours watching her and learning the basics. At the age of nine, I offered to do the family dinner, and mum was bold enough to give me an opportunity. It was fish stew and rice. I took to cooking like a fish to water, and it is a passion that I have carried well into adulthood, hence why you have enjoyed a delightful meal tonight.

The early years of my life were shaped by the sounds of freedom, loudness of speech, diverse dialects spoken around me daily, the joys of playing outdoors fearlessly, the fragrance of freshly cooked meals, laughter in our home, dogs barking, cows mooing, chickens clucking, frequent trips to the beach where the power of the ocean, and the endless lashing of the waves on the shore, which never ceased to amaze me. In the midst of it all, I recognised that I was privileged to have been born into a family of loving parents who put the wellbeing of their children first. We went to private schools and had the best our parents could afford. We lived in a house built by my dad, and I loved the privacy of stealing away into my room into a place I called my own.

When I had disagreements with my brothers, to avoid the conflict, I would go and talk to my teddies or play with my dolls or do whatever I wanted in that space that was mine. We were taught to respect each other's space, and I learnt to love my space and value the benefit of my alone time—that gave me time to dream. When I would go off the rails, my dad would send me to my room to think about my indiscretions and boy, how those times of 'punishment' created a place for me to dream. My mum, being the disciplinarian, had a different approach. I would lock myself away and let my imagination run wild. I would dream of things I would create, the way I wanted to live, how I wanted to be a success, and almost always, get trapped in a castle and be rescued by my knight in shining armour.

My daydreams were often of me all grown up and being extremely successful in whatever I had chosen to do to and always being happily married to the man of my dreams with a loving family. I had an innate maternal streak that was demonstrated in how I cared for my brothers and stepped into my mum's role with unarguable leadership qualities in the responsibilities I was given whenever she was away.

At a very young age, our parents drummed the principle of The Golden Rule, to treat others as you would love to be treated, in our hearts. I grew up being sensitive to other people's needs and learnt to respect the fact that one man's meat is another man's poison. I played fairly with the children in the neighbourhood, had good friends at school, and actively stayed away from trouble. Sometimes however, trouble seemed to follow me. Once, for example, while the first house we lived in was being built, my dad chose a room to store building materials. On numerous occasions, we were told to never go into that room, without being told why. Somehow, once when we were left on site, out of sheer curiosity, I found myself leading the pack wandering into the 'forbidden' room. As we looked around, we realised that all that was in the room was cement bags, building tools, and pipes. Suddenly, the door slammed shut, locking us in the room. Only then did we realise that the lock was faulty from the inside, disallowing us to be let out.

I freaked out and burst out crying. My older brother, Joe, remembering that our grandmother always says, "Prayer Changes things," ordered us to kneel in reverence to God and led us in prayer –starting with a confession for our disobedience. He asked us to pray and to shout loudly, so God could hear. Nothing happened! We shouted, beat the door, sat in isolation, contemplating our fate until Jesse, my other brother, realised that he could dismantle the lock with a screw driver, which he had seen in a toolbox. Alas! We were freed! Once we were let out, he rebuilt the lock again before our parents returned. Had we been in that room until our parents had returned, well, prayers would have been needed to change things.

On another occasion while in primary school, I walked onto the playground to find a boy bullying Joe. I pounced on him, beat him black and blue, and stuffed his mouth with leaves, an incident that landed me at the Head Teacher's office and detention for the rest of the week.

Despite being the only girl and petite with a small frame,

I was a tomboy at a young age. I was extremely close to my dad whom I absolutely adored for how he set an example of what an honourable man should be. In my father's house, I felt safe, secure, protected, provided for, and nurtured with hope for a brilliant future. Dad and I had a good rapport, and there was the liberty to talk to him about everything and anything. In Africa, where corporal punishment is a norm rather than senseless physical punishment, dad reasoned with me over my indiscretions, mishaps, misbehaviours, growth spurts tantrums, and hormonal adjustments. I saw him treat mum well, and he taught my brothers to respect women and to be law abiding citizens and honourable men of tomorrow.

I went for sunset rides with him and we would talk about life—sharing lots of nuggets of wisdom that have helped me through life in decision making and crisis, giving me an insight into seemingly difficult situations.

In our house, there were no taboos. Our parents were open with us about the facts of life, freedom of choice, actions, and consequences. Our father took time to parent us especially in the teenage years; he would take me to the movies, take me out for meals, take me for long sunset drives, and have heart-to-heart conversations with me about life. He explained to me about boys and how they operate— knowledge that equipped me with the will to stay a virgin until the day I got married. He helped me understand about the power of choice I had as a woman,—that I may not like every experience I face in life, but my success was dependent on how well I handled what he referred to as 'the degree of disappointment.'

This concept is the disparity between the ideal perception

of an experience and the reality of the actual experience. Dad helped me understand that people evolve in life, and in order to stay relevant to any person sharing the journey of life, one has got to evolve with them; otherwise they will fall off like dead skin. It's almost like riding on a motorcycle with someone. As they go around the bends, you have got to lean in with them otherwise you will fall off in the turns of life. He helped me understand that he loved our mother, and he had learnt to fall in love with her many times over the changing scenes of life. Through our relationship, I developed a high expectation of what love should look and feel like and how I wanted to be treated by my future husband. I faced life with optimism, drive, and principle.

I grew up with high aspirations and expectations. Living in Africa had it challenges. Even though we were being raised upper middle class, we endured some hardships that befell the nation. There were times when food was scarce, fuel was in short supply, or quite simply, the nation struggled with basic amenities of life as a result of poor leadership. For a period of time, our parents worked away from home, and we had to live with our grandparents, sharing time and space with our cousins, whose parents also travelled for work or study. I realised at a very young age that I am quite accommodating and really love people. I appreciate the beauty in the diversity of life, and that always intrigued me.

My determination to realise the dreams of my childhood made me a very strong-willed, dynamic, go-getter who is passionate yet passively aggressive about fulfilling destiny. However, when the chips are down, there is a little girl inside of me that desires to love and be loved in a way that will fulfil my human need for love.

The first person I was close friends with was a girl next door who was my oracle for all things streetwise. Rebecca, despite being the same age as me, was much more mature and knowledgeable in my eyes. My childhood friend, Rebecca was from one of the provincial tribes and by no means had the comforts nor was cushioned to face life like I was. We would take raw ingredients from our mother's kitchens to cook in a makeshift kitchen we built at the back of our house. She taught me traditional dances, and in many ways, our conversations took us outside the confines and safety of the sheltered life my parents had created for us.

Rebecca had one brother, and I had three—four boys that clearly did not want the girls 'cramping their style' or sharing their company. So naturally, this deepened the bond between us both. Sometimes when I was naughty and sent to my room—grounded for a period, she would run around the house and find my room window to play with me from the outside through the window. I longed to go home daily from school to hear of her day's experiences and share mine.

On December 26, Boxing Day, as was common in Sierra Leone, both families took a trip to the beach. Sierra Leone lies on the West Coast of Africa and is bordered on the west by the Atlantic Ocean. There are a number of pristine beaches along the peninsula, and a family day-out to any of the beaches on public holidays were a common practice. There were two major activities that usually took place on Boxing Day: a national athletics event commonly called Boxing Day Sports or various family beach outings. It so happened to be Rebecca's mum's birthday, and she had friends over, so she declined to make the beach trip as did my mum who opted to spend time with her. Both dads took the kids plus a cousin of mine who lived in the neighbourhood in two cars. As we left, both mothers shouted out "don't get into the ocean guys! You know you all can't swim well. Swimming in a pool and swimming in the ocean are two different things so don't y'all dare get in the ocean!"

We got to the beach and played on the shore, building sandcastles for a bit while the dads lounged on beach chairs and indulged in adult chitchat over chilled drinks. Suddenly as if pulled by a magnetic force, Rebecca undressed in a jiffy and ran into the ocean. Relentlessly, she battered the waves as she entered and went in knee deep, waist deep, neck deep until suddenly she was swept up by a giant wave. She disappeared momentarily underneath the wave and resurfaced further into the ocean. Everyone was in such deep shock, and I certainly was yet again in deep awe of the power of the waves as a cloud of confusion filled my mind.

At that moment, a seed of fear was sown—I feared losing my best friend; I feared drowning by some unexplained means. I wondered how the ocean can be so inspiring yet so unforgiving. I just feared. I screamed Rebecca's name over and over, but my voice was drowned by the crowd of people who had congregated and were freaking out over realising a young ten-year old girl was battling the angry ocean. She came up and yelled for help before she was encapsulated by yet another wave and disappeared momentarily again. The frenzy of her struggle had spread like wildfire, and competent swimmers on the shore ran into the ocean to get her out. I stood in complete shock and watched her screaming and disappearing. Before she could be reached, she went under with another giant wave and never came back up. A cold shiver went down my spine. The water was quickly evacuated as the tides had changed and were clearly angry and unrelenting. Trained rescue swimmers frantically searched the rough waters for a good while before concluding that maybe she had drowned. I was in utter disbelief—cold to the bone with unquantifiable and total shock. Suddenly, I had a sense of unexplained emptiness. My friend, my confidant, the sister I had always wanted, was suddenly snatched from me? The next few hours were a blur. How does a ten-year old deal with the death of her best friend who was well and in good health. Who was building sandcastles one minute and was gone the next?

The dads decided to drive us home while professional divers were called to continue searching for her. On returning without Rebecca, her mum's birthday gathering turned completely sour. Africans are very emotionally demonstrative, and the contemplation of the fact that Rebecca was no more, consumed the neighbourhood within minutes. News like this travels like wildfire, and women came from far and wide, renting their clothes, pulling their hair, and wailing. I was numb. I couldn't cry. I couldn't think. Rebecca's mum was inconsolable! She rent her clothes and rolled on the dirt. This was her birthday, and she was facing every mother's worst nightmare. The sound of the wailing women went late into the night.

My brothers and I were hastily ushered to bed while the dads returned to the beach. I lay staring into the ceiling thinking over and over and over that surely Rebecca can't just die! "I am sure they will find her, please God let them find her," I muttered over and over. Little did I know that for someone to be in the ocean that long, the likelihood of being found alive was very, very slim. I waited in hope for the dads to return with good news from the divers' search. The father's did come back after midnight in tears and dejection that indeed Rebecca had indeed drowned. I lay in bed alone and did not sleep a wink, reminiscing of the conversations we had and the times we had shared.

To a ten-year old, losing a best friend in such a tragic manner makes no sense. The next day, the search continued, and it took 3 days for Rebecca's corpse to be found. My grief was personalised, intense, and indescribable. All the adults were so grief stricken and so desperately in need of answers that no one stopped to think of what I might be going through. In the months that followed, I sat alone, played alone, and in my own way, over time, came to terms with the fact that I will no longer see my friend.

Somehow, I was so stunned and numb from this experience that I couldn't and never allowed myself to shed a tear—for years. My parents decided not to allow me to attend her funeral. My mum did not want me to see her in a coffin, but I sneaked and peeped while she was being laid for a viewing. She was dark, much darker than I had known her to be, swollen to almost 3 times her size, and her eyes, ears, and nose were momentarily dripping with the water that had saturated her body. This image stuck in my mind and deepened my personal pain. I felt there was no time to say goodbye.

As time progressed, I stopped taking baths, only showers as every time I was submerged in a tub, I had flashbacks of Rebecca drowning. I hated any bathroom that was decorated with a sea life motif. Rebecca's death had changed me in a way I did not fully understand. That solid framework of psychological security my parents had worked so hard to give me was dented and nobody realised, not even me, as I continued life as normal.

A few of years after Rebecca's death, my family moved into a house in a new neighbourhood—interestingly by the ocean, and I had an opportunity to go to a new school and make new friends.

At 14, I started a new secondary school much closer to the new neighbourhood. After I did the entrance assessment, it was decided jointly by both teachers and my parents that I repeat the year I had just completed. Math (which turned out to be my favourite subject) was particularly weak, and since at that time I was eyeing a career with science biases, it was the best thing for me. The grading system back in the day would average the marks of the individual test scores, and student reports clearly indicated how well they were doing in relation to their peers. So there would be someone who would be 1st, 2nd, 3rd etc., and if at the end of the year, one doesn't make the pass grade of at least 50% on average of all subjects, they will need to repeat the year. There is much stigma of failure attached to that. So when I found myself needing to repeat a year, I had to deal with the feelings of failure as I knew I was not stupid, and I did not have the opportunity to explain to the world that I made the grade to the next year, but I needed to strengthen my math.

Thankfully, I gravitated to and was 'accepted' into the clique of the most studious group of girls in the school. This was an all-girls, Christian boarding school that had very high standards. I was a day student, however. I blossomed academically and made really good grades. There was a friendly and fierce competition among the 'super-six'—the name given to our group as we were such high achievers. I loved this school. I felt a belonging and an acceptance that was lacking in my life since Rebecca passed.

I had an aptitude for sports and excelled in track and field. At 15, I competed in the inter-secondary school competition where I effortlessly smashed the national 200m record and made it into the national team. Every single day after school, I would go the National Stadium and train with the other national athletes.

While in that school, I also realised my gift for public speaking, and I was privileged to compete in the annual inter-secondary school debates and won many times over. I carried myself with class and was a very eloquent woman in the making. At prize-giving ceremonies, which were an annual event held at schools to recognise and celebrate academic achievement, I had the opportunity of representing the English department several times, compering the ceremony and acting in the school plays. I won the best actress award two years in a row and several other academic prizes. I seemed to have the Midas touch and the future sure seemed so bright.

It was commonplace to have nicknames in Sierra Leone, and often, they were not complimentary. Even though the nicknames were given in jest, I refused to allow anyone to call me anything that was not edifying or was not complimentary.

One day at school as I was walking across the compound at lunch, I heard singing from the school hall and decided to check out what was going on. When I entered, I saw a small group of students and a couple of teachers. It was quite an unusual meeting as they were singing hymns and Christian spiritual songs. At the end of the singing, there was a short teaching on the love of God and His desire for a personal and intimate relationship with mankind. The speaker explained that all humans were born physically alive but spiritually dead in desperate need of a saviour and a need to be awakened spiritually and be reconnected back to God.

At age nine at a social BBQ event of a church, I had heard a similar message, it warmed my heart and resonated with me. In spite of the seeming way in which my life was blossoming, I had questions on eternity and God in general, so it was soul-stirring to hear someone who did not know me personally speak to the questions I had. At the end of the meeting, the speaker invited all who desired to have that relationship with God through the Lordship of Jesus to step forward. I and a few others took that step. For me, it was a life changing moment. I said a prayer, acknowledging my need for a saviour and invited Jesus to be my Lord. I proposed to get to know Christ in a personal way, and this decision would become another significant pillar in my life. There was no lightening or anything dramatic, yet deep inside of me, I knew a change had taken place, and I now belong to Jesus.

I found a vibrant local church and got a Bible. I started reading it and making its principles my yardstick for life. I continued training and competing athletically and decided to let everything about my life bring glory to God. Most of the churches back then were led by people who felt they 'had a calling' into the office of a pastor without sometimes proper or thorough theological training. As a result, there were many man-made doctrines that seem to somewhat bring people in bondage rather than give them the liberty that Christ died to give them.

Personally, I was experiencing great peace, a joy that the world could not take from me and a quiet assurance of the

Fatherhood of God. Neither my family nor my friends could understand my passion for this new relationship I had found. I had a clear sense of liberty, but there was a lot of conflict in finding my place in the church as in the local assembly I was attached to, there was a lot of emphasis on what a Christian should look like rather than who a Christian should be. I, on the other hand, was a free spirited, fun loving, young girl that could not easily be 'tamed.' Nonetheless, my enthusiasm was contagious. I shared my faith at any opportunity I had and passionately embraced the doctrines of the Bible. I caught on very early about the importance of the condition of the heart and that God is more concerned that we are 'right' within rather than an outward show of holiness.

Just before I turned 15, I went driving with dad along the beachfront in one of our heart-to-heart conversations about life and love. I had never had a boyfriend at that point but sure was curious about what love would be like for me. I questioned my dad endlessly on love. He patiently answered my questions and lightened the mood by explaining that boys have two brains—one in their heads and one in their pants. In their teens and sometimes through life, the brain in their pants are more active and make more decisions than the one in their heads.

My dad gave me an insight into how men think and how they operate—a knowledge that helped me navigate many treacherous waters and helped me see through many guys. In one conversation, I told my dad that I desired to preserve my virginity to the day I get married, and my dad supported the idea. He commended me on that decision and assured me that it was a noble resolution. He told me that I did not have control over the day I was born nor may I over the day

I die, but I do have control over what I do in between and more importantly, over what I choose to do with my body.

I then said "Daddy, when you walk me down the aisle on my wedding day, if I look at you and wink before you hand me over to my husband to be, please know I have kept my resolve. If not, forgive me, for I may have experienced a moment of weakness, but I do value your voice in my life and treasure your support for my decisions. Thanks for the insights you have given me."

My dad then said, "If per chance, you find yourself in a situation beyond your control and inadvertently fall pregnant, come to us and let us deal with it as a family. Don't ever try and do something stupid like have an abortion."

That conversation was so deep to me I could even recollect the shirt daddy wore that day. We hugged, and I went home from that conversation fully committed to celibacy until marriage. The drive home was so quiet. My brain was in full throttle as I processed and digested the conversation.

First Love

At age 15, I was making my way home from school on a familiar path that was common to me when I noticed a new guy in the neighbourhood. He stood with arms folded, with a coy and cheeky smile, standing seemingly aimlessly. "Hey!" he said as I drew closer, nodding his head, "Do you live around here?"

I felt a tug in my tummy and stood speechless, trying to look indifferent and unconcerned. "Well hell yeah! Why?" I said defensively. "What else will I be doing around here if not going home?" I desperately tried to look away from his piercing eyes as realised I was experiencing a range of emotions that were intriguing and unfamiliar but exciting.

This guy was so incredibly handsome and rugged. I was massively attracted to him. At most, he was no more than a couple of years older than me. "Would it be okay if I walk you home?" he asked, completely ignoring my attempts to be indifferent.

"Sure," I replied, feeling rather powerless at the range of emotions I was experiencing.

"I'm Leo." he said as we walked along, "I must admit, you are amazingly beautiful, and it is my joy not to complete my homework today but to ensure no stray dog or wild animal attack you on your way home and that neither a wasp nor a bumble bee stings you. You are too precious, and I feel I need to protect you."

I chuckled, introduced myself, and we chatted happily as he walked me home.

Strangely, I felt like I had known him all my life. Within 15 minutes, we were at my home, and he gave me a big, lingering hug, which I did not resist. I felt like a million dollars as I skipped upstairs to greet my mum and to get on with the activities of my afternoon. Somehow, coincidentally, Leo was at the same spot the next day and daily thereafter as I walked home. He became a familiar face and a dependable companion. Slowly as we chatted, he became a confidant. One day on the journey home, Leo asked that we share a kiss before getting to my house gate. I blushed as I consented. It was magical! I felt waves of passion bursting from my heart all the way to my toes.

Wow, I must be in love! I thought. This is the most amazing thing ever. I twirled and danced and skipped, whistling and humming love songs along with the radio. I was in a state of total euphoria for days. I was experiencing letting my heart go for the first time. In my eyes, Leo was a dream come true. I did not go looking for him, but he found me. When I mined his heart, it was a treasure box—full of precious jewels.

He was strong, handsome, intelligent, kind, tender, and sincere. He did not put a foot wrong. On occasion, he would carry me on his back if I was weary. We shared many passionate kisses, deep secrets, and the joy of companionship that was only fully understood by us both. This euphoric first love experience went on for a year. Leo bonded with my brothers, was embraced by my parents, and became an extension to my family. He would often join us for meals and share in any significant family occasions. In my little 15-year old mind, I planned a wedding with Leo and daydreamed of how many children we would have together, what castle we would live in, and how Leo would forever be the prince among men in my eyes.

We became study mates, went to the beach together in the evenings, and effortlessly developed a bond that was seemingly unbreakable. Like any boy his age, however, Leo wanted to explore his sexual fantasies, which directly conflicted with my convictions and resolve. I had shared my faith with him, and it didn't faze him that I was a practising Christian and as a result, had commitments that I was not willing to compromise on. One day, he invited me over to his house and gave me a packet of condoms for 'safe keeping.' I had never seen or handled condoms before. He told me, "no matter what you do, don't let your dad see these."

"What are they?" I asked.

"Something special we will need sometime in the future," he replied. I went home and asked Joe, my older brother, about the mysterious package.

He went ballistic. "Did he touch you?" he asked.

"We always touch each other. Why are you so agitated?" I innocently asked. "I like stroking his face. He gives me back rubs—What do you mean?"

"I mean did he have sex with you, dummy!"

"Oh no! He knows I want to wait." I said

"So why the hell did he give you these? Let me take care of this joker." Joe exclaimed and dashed out of the house, looking enraged like a wounded animal. I was quite baffled as I thought they were balloons when he had taken them out of their packaging.

He came back looking more composed and declared, "He will not dare mess with you; I have made sure of that. Give me the package let me get rid of it."

Later that evening, Leo asked that we meet at the end of the drive leading to my house. I walked out to meet him, and he held me as he looked into my eyes. For the first time, he was at a loss for words.

"Are you OK?" I asked.

"Well your brother has threatened to kill me if I hurt you."

"But you haven't hurt me." I replied.

"It's about the package I gave you—Avril, they are condoms."

I felt betrayed, confused and grossly misunderstood. "I thought I told you I want us to wait," I said.

"Yeah, but I'm burning. We are too young to get married, and maybe if you would, well allow me, I promise I will never leave you. I really don't want to hurt you, and I certainly don't want Joe to kill me."

"Leo!" I screamed as I burst into tears. "What's wrong with you? You want me to get pregnant and to drop out of school? It's over! You told me you will wait, and now, you want me to sleep with you? Come on Leo, this was not the deal!"

"Avril," he said with his voice calm and composed, "I love you. I just want us to take things to the next level. I am not sure I can wait anymore. I don't want your brother thinking that I want to hurt you. You are precious to me, and I do want to be with you. Let me come clean. I know I cannot continue to pretend that I will not want to sleep with you. I am sure we can work through this."

I ran off crying, all the way home and straight to my room, slammed my door, buried my face in my pillow, and cried until there were no more tears left. In my heart, I knew we had come to a major crossroad, and I was not willing to compromise.

In the days that followed, Leo was a no show. It was becoming evident to me that my fairy tale was fast dissipating. I couldn't understand how and why things had changed so quickly. My heart felt like it was literally, physically being shattered. I took my guitar to the beach after school when I had the time and just strummed chords as tears fell down my face. It was like the light was taken from my world. I went to visit Leo after a few days, and he wouldn't come out of his room to meet me. I went home and cried.

One day, my dad came home and met me in a complete meltdown. Somehow everyone knew that things with Leo were not going good but did not know why or what had happened except Joe. He had been in and out of relationships at this point, and his only consolation for me was, "You will get over him. I knew it. I know all he wanted was to sleep with you!"

After a few days, my dad came to my room, sat next to me on the bed with his arms around me and said, "Its Leo, isn't it?"

I burst out crying afresh as I exclaimed, "Daddy, it's over, I think we have broken up."

My dad rocked me gently as he allowed me to face the painful reality that indeed my fairy tale might be over. When my sobbing subsided, he said, "Baby girl, look at me. I want to teach you something. If you love a bird, let it fly. If it comes back to you, then it is surely yours. If it doesn't, it never was yours to start off with. Well maybe if it does comes back, nobody wanted it so you might as well let it go again."

We both burst out laughing.

"I don't know what has happened between you both, but maybe you ought to let Leo go for a season. If he is yours, he will come back to you." I felt a surge of hope pierce the sense of pain I had felt for days. I decided to let Leo 'fly' and trusted God to bring him back.

He never came back. In fact, he left for university and rarely came home. The intensity of the loss and the pain of the heartache I felt eased as days turned into months and months into years. However, he forever remained special to me.

I continued to apply myself academically and progressed through 6th form. As one progressed up the educational ladder, it became more challenging with scarcity of books and of availability of suitably qualified teachers. There was only one university in Sierra Leone offering some very limited degree courses. For people who long to further their education diversely, it was important that they are either sent abroad as students by their parents or earn a scholarship to cater for tuition and living expenses at a foreign university.

At the end of my A Levels, I decide to pursue a diploma in IT, an area that I seemingly stumbled into while exploring the possibility of studying abroad. The circumstances in our family life had changed dramatically, and my parents at this point could not pay for me to pursue my dreams, so I needed a miracle.

Our family was well off, yet we were met with a lot of challenges that impacted my personal perspectives. Rewinding to when I was about 11 years old, my parents decided on building a house. After a season of working away from home, they got a plot of land on a hill with amazing views. In a short space of time, the house was completed and was very beautiful. It was so good to have a place that I could call home and that I was proud to have friends over at. It was carpeted throughout, fully air conditioned, and had 'luxuries' such as a washing machine, which was a rarity in those days.

However, one day during our school mid-term break, tragedy struck! My parents did not want me to stay home alone, so they asked that I go spend some time with my grandmother. I was very reluctant because in my grandma's house, kids work! So the thought of spending my half-term break in hard labour, really put me off. I tried, as I had done on a number of occasions, to play my parents against each other. I waited until my mum went to have her morning shower, and I went in to see my dad with my usual 'puppy dog eyes,' pleading to stay home.

My mum came back into their bedroom as she needed to get something and met me in action, negotiating my way out of going to grandma's. Then, the penny dropped as dad asked me whether mum had agreed to me staying, and I had emphatically said yes. Only, she had not. My dad then realised what I had done and ordered me to go get ready for grandma's. My parents asked me to get dressed and even though she was a 10-minute walk away, offered to drop me off.

I promised them I would walk there, and they phoned her to let her know I was on my way. Then, they left for work. I got ready and headed down the road, walking as slowly as I possibly could. As I was entering her house, I heard her screaming on the phone, then she dropped it in relief with tears in her eyes. She ran over and hugged me tightly as she repeatedly said, "thank you Jesus, thank you Jesus!"

I was bewildered to say the least.

Then she said, "There has been an accident. A lorry lost control coming down the hill and has flattened half your house. We were all worried because we thought you were still at home. Bricks and mortar can be replaced, but your life dear girl . . . ." She couldn't finish the statement. She shook her head and wiped tears from her eyes.

I couldn't understand. She asked her driver to pull out her car, so we can go back to our house to see what had happened. We went back to our house, and I couldn't believe my eyes. This couldn't be the same place I had left 10 mins before. There was a tipper parked in the living room with its bonnet out in the veranda. I walked in and gingerly walked around. I realised God had saved me from a certain death.

There were cracks in the walls throughout the house. Our beautiful home was destroyed. That incident started a season of hardships in our family. It was just one thing after another. We had to live in the half-broken house for a while. This was the same house we lived in after Rebecca's drowning incident, and that accident was the catalyst for our house move.

When we moved to the house by the beach, it was another one built by my dad, but we moved in before the house was finished. I was so very proud of my dad—how he summoned the courage and strength to face the adversity of losing his home yet went on to build another one twice its size. I learnt a lesson right there—tenacity in the face of adversity. I watched my parents fend for us even though I was well-aware things were not always easy financially. Our parents were such selfless and sacrificial givers.

My dad was a university-qualified and experientially-skilled mechanical engineer. He had always had good jobs and brought home the bacon, giving us all we ever needed. However, about the time I finished 6th form, he had some difficulties at work and had to leave his job. He assumed he would find something else quickly, but one door after another closed, and I watched him go through having to hold the family together in spite of the unemployment situation. He had limited savings, and there were so many luxuries we had to cut back on.

Again, I learnt how important a man's job is to him and how a man's ego could be impacted by what he does and his ability to effectively look after his family.

So when I finished 6th form, I pursued a diploma at a college institute while thinking through my next steps. When I completed the diploma in IT, I landed some juicy opportunities and easily started making almost what my dad had last earned at 18 years of age. This helped a lot financially at home and boy did I begin to see the rewards. I learnt another lesson at this point—givers never lack. As part of the opportunities I had, I was asked to teach a certificate course to preliminary students who were going for the diploma I had just completed. This was a role I did not take seriously at all. One day, the Director of the Institute was asked to nominate some recent graduates from the Diploma Programme to be awarded a scholarship to study abroad.

I was one of those nominated, and I did not even know as I had not shown up to work for a few days. The Director then sent his messenger out to go look for me. Freetown is a pretty small city; however, it was just by stroke of luck that this man, the messenger, happened to be roaming around the town centre, when he stumbled on me. "Director" (as he was fondly referred to) "would like to see you," he said.

I must be in big trouble, I thought. I went back with this guy and hesitantly walked up to the Director's office.

"Where in the hell have you been? I have been looking for you all over the damn place!" Director blurted out.

"I am sorry Director. I have been caught up with some personal bits and pieces." I responded stuttering slightly.

"Listen girl. You young folks these days are not serious. But you girl, you are special! I have received a few scholarships, and you have been nominated to be one of our recipients. Some folks will go to India, and some will go to Japan, and your lot will meet again in England."

I couldn't believe it. He said it in such a matter of fact way.

I had to find somewhere to sit. "So which group would I be going with?" Almost thinking this was a cruel joke.

He continued very seriously. "You are with the group that will be going to India. This is the only year I have received these and girl, it might be the last. This government does not have these favours easily. You better go and shine. Get you affairs in order, you should be leaving in three months' time." He handed me a document detailing the logistics.

I couldn't get home quickly enough to tell the family. That trip home was interesting. I sat in a taxi and just soaked in the views, knowing I will soon be leaving my family and the place I have called home.

My joy and excitement were laced with peace that God answers prayers. I had such mixed feelings. I felt honoured to have been chosen—this was certainly an answer to prayer. Where else would I have had this breakthrough from? I was indescribably excited as I approached home, knowing my life was about to change forever! I screamed so loudly when I got to the house gate, that my mum thought something had happened to me. She came running out to meet me. I started dancing, and she joined me, knowing that obviously I had good news; although, she did not know what I had to say.

Everyone left what they were doing and congregated in the living room as we would often do when there is big news. "I have been awarded a scholarship, and I am leaving in 3 months!" I blurted out. The whole house erupted. There was so much jubilation. We sat down as we had done many nights as a family and were so thankful. It dawned on me that God does work in mysterious ways. If I had not repeated the year group at school when I moved schools, I will not have been in the year that the scholarships were made available and academically ready (having completed the diploma) to be awarded one.

I had daydreamed about what I'd be up to and how at 18, I was about to fly the nest and be all grown up. The future seemed so bright. I started winding down my affairs. I began to spend quality time with friends and took time to travel around and create mental snapshots of the various places. I knew it would take ages before I returned, so I made the most of those three months.

One day, a friend of mine in the neighbourhood asked me if I would help his cousin, who was visiting from the UK, to type up his thesis. He was reading his Masters in Economics at Oxford University in England. He was quite in desperate need of administrative help as he had a lot on his plate, so he was willing to pay whatever I asked. I had some time on my hands, so I decided to meet up with him and help out for a small fee of course.

We planned to meet at an office that turned out to be his mum's business. I walked into the office and was completely smitten by this guy, Rick. In my eyes he was the epitome of everything I had dreamt my ideal man would look like. He was about 6'2, fair in complexion as he had racially mixed parentage, his lips were baby pink, and he had the most perfect set of teeth I had seen. His deep-set eyes were hazel, and his hair was soft, curly and jet black. His hands were large and comforting, and there was such a self-assurance about him that was undeniable.

He strode with confidence and spoke with such conviction in what he said. His baritone voice was mesmerising, and it was hard not to notice his well-chiselled body under his t-shirt. I was totally unprepared for the effect he had on me. I was actually breathless and totally speechless. That same tingling that I experienced with Leo so many years ago came back. I said hello and started shaking. I actually became weak at the knees. Rick shook my hand, and my palm was sweating. Funny thing is that this had never happened to me before—I had never experienced sweaty palms! I must have looked a right state because he asked if I would like a drink and a place to sit.

As he walked away to get me a can of chilled 7UP, I told myself to regain my composure. It was surreal. Could it be I am falling in love again? What was this? Rick explained what he needed me to type up and when he needed it by. I couldn't look at his face lest I give away my instant and unquestionable attraction. I had already given much away, so I had to leave before making a complete fool of myself.

Just as I was putting my things together to leave, he reached out and held my shoulder. I looked up at his eyes almost questioning within myself if he had read my body language. It seemed like eternity that we locked eyes, and then, he asked me if I would like to have lunch with him the following week. "It will be my delight." I responded, grinning from ear to ear. I took his file of loose sheets, scribbled notes, and left hastily, questioning myself whether my makeup, outfit, and hair were on point for such a momentous occasion.

I went home and met Jesse, my brother who had to endure my endless repertoire of this amazing guy. I gave him an earful. He was quite intrigued and decided to spy on my lunch date to see who this mystery guy was.

The following Tuesday could not come soon enough.

I got dressed super tastefully and promised myself that none of the attraction nerves will kick in! There was no way I was going to behave like a little kid in a candy store. I approached the restaurant we had planned to meet at, and there he was—Prince Charming stood waiting for me. As soon as he saw me, he had the warmest smile. He gave me a hug and thanked me for making time to dine with him. In my head, I was like *Are you kidding me? I should be thanking you! I am sure all the girls in this town would like a lunch date with you and you are thanking me?*

We sat down to eat and chose our various meals. As we ate, I realised Rick was quite short with the staff and snapped rudely if he wanted something that wasn't readily brought. I was put off by his arrogance. I wasn't raised to disrespect people no matter their status in life. I also realised he was a chain smoker. He was losing points fast, but he was still very charming with me, and we had good rapport. Unlike the first meeting, I was surprisingly relaxed, and we spoke effortlessly. It was evident we were both attracted to each other. We decided to meet again. I had a couple of months to leave Sierra Leone, how was I going to manage this tug on my heart?

As we continued to hang out, he opened up to me, and it was so beautiful to experience a macho man, who was so strong, intelligent, and so well rounded, soften up and be vulnerable. I shared my faith and how that helped me when Leo and I broke up. I felt blessed and privileged to be his confidant. He told me he wanted to stop smoking and wanted to go to church with me. We took trips to the beach and grew to be really fond of each other. I finished the thesis and handed it back to him, refusing payment. At the time of the completion of the thesis, he had taken me out so many times that it would have been really awkward. He insisted and told me of how much he valued my time and that it was a matter of principle.

We had a business arrangement, and he wanted to honour the deal. That impressed me. Even though we had not established a relationship, we were practically in one. He told me of someone he was seeing in England and that things were not working out. His time in Sierra Leone had helped him put things in perspective, and he really wanted to see how things would evolve between us. I was sceptical about the other girl and more so that he was returning to England to an apartment they shared. We had an amazing time though, and I really liked Rick as a person. Somehow, I couldn't permit my heart to fall for him completely.

It would have complicated things for me. Once when he asked me to hang out with him at his home, his mum came to find us frolicking in the living room. The look of displeasure on her face was so intense. She called Rick to one of the rooms, and I could hear him being scolded for nurturing a holiday romance. He kept telling her, "Mum, I have feelings for this girl. This is not just a holiday thing." His mum clearly felt he should try and work things out with his ex, and to my dismay, she said some very uncomplimentary things about "local girls in Sierra Leone" within which she had categorised me. Little did they both realise I overheard the whole conversation. That really put a damper on me, and I nurtured the courage to tell him I was leaving with a couple of weeks' notice. He was devastated. It was only then I realised I had been knitting bonds with him too, and it wasn't easy for me either.

The three months from the date I was notified of my scholarship award quickly went by, and I was boarding a plane on my own to face the world for the first time. My family came to see me off at the airport and boy, was I emotional. I had the feeling of being detached from 'my familiar.' It was exciting yet scary. I had such mixed feelings. Finally, as I climbed the stairs with 3 of my former classmates on to the aircraft that was bound for France where we were going to have our visas for India processed, I looked back one last time and blew a goodbye kiss to my past as I waved frantically to my family. I resolved not to waste my life. That walk to my seat was so strategic for me. I was positioning myself for change, for elevation, and for success. I was barely 18 years old. Young, impressionable, inexperienced, I was armed with a determined mind and strong values from my upbringing. I had such strong love for my family, but my destiny was pulling me to fulfilment.

India

I was knocked out during the six-hour flight to Paris, having been totally emotionally drained by the euphoric build up to and departure from home. I was at a window seat on the plane, and we landed in Paris at the crack of dawn. As the plane descended into Charles de Gaulle airport, I looked outside the window. What a beautiful city it was from the sky! I totally fell in love with Paris.

We spent a few days in a hotel and had to commute around in this foreign city. It was all so very exciting. We got our Indian visas sorted and tied up our affairs in Paris. We left on a 13-hour flight to New Delhi. Again, due to physical, emotional, and mental fatigue, I slept through most of it. However, as the plane landed, I woke up again and looked out as we flew over the Himalayas Mountain ranges. It was so breath taking that I will never forget it as long as I live. The sun was rising, and it seemed to literally come from under the earth. It was indescribably beautiful.

India was an experience. I ate foods I didn't know existed and was mesmerised by the sights and sounds of such a culturally rich nation. I shared a room with a former classmate, and on this exchange programme, there were 42 students from different countries around the world. We had one thing in common: a desire to be the next generation leaders in IT as an industry sector. My desire for knowledge and aptitude for learning was insatiable and unequalled. I constantly thought about where I came from, and apart from my beautiful family, there was not much to go back to, so I had to take advantage of the opportunities I had been presented and to maximize my potential.

We had a lot of classes and workshops with an institute that pulled together the high achievers from various institutions and universities. It was such an interesting and eye-opening experience to realise how academically astute the Indians are. I met a bunch of very driven young men and women who had success in mind and were hungrily in pursuit of it. At the end of the year, we were awarded a diploma that will serve as the access course we would need for our next phase at University. While I was in India, I attracted a lot of attention, but none of the guys rocked my boat. In one instance, one of the guys who was assigned to ensure we are taken care of seized my passport and threatened to stop me from leaving if I did not declare my (non-existent) undying love for him. It was all in jest, and he made me chuckle so many times. It was great to be away from home and to be experiencing such fun with perfect strangers. My horizon was being broadened in a beautiful way.

To give us a well-rounded experience, the institution organised tours for us to places of interest. We went to various Buddhist temples, including the famous Lotus Temple, visited the Taj Ma Hall, and had a go at mountain climbing in one of the ranges of the Himalayas. It was the scariest thing that I had ever put myself through. We climbed over 2000 feet and camped at one of the bases for a day. That was another experience that will be hard to forget. When I stood on the plateau, there was nothing but mountain ranges as far as my eyes could see. My heart burst forth with praises to God, and I realised that in size, we are insignificant in this universe.

The greatest challenge I had was with that of hygiene. I found New Delhi exceptionally filthy. Coming from Africa, I had seen poverty first-hand, but the extent of poverty in India was heart breaking. The dominant religion in India is Hinduism that deifies cows, so Hindus do not eat meat. This was particularly difficult for us. One day, one of the other delegates on our program said he had found a place where we could get meat. That there were some Muslim butchers he had stumbled on that could sell us some meat.

We went with this guy to the 'meat market,' which happened to be located miles away in the slums under a disused bridge. Little did it occur to us that buying produce from a place that unhygienic was this was an absolute recipe for disaster. Anyway, we bought a good chunk of meat and went to another market, bought a ring burner and a little non-stick pot. We lived in a 5-star hotel, so it goes without saying that due to health and safety regulations, it was not permitted for us to cook in our rooms, but necessity became the mother of invention. We cooked stew with the meat and ordered some rice by room service.

Soon after the meal was finished, within a matter of hours, everyone who ate began to feel sick. We were throwing up all over the place, coupled with diarrhoea. We called the emergency services, and an ambulance came and took us to hospital. I became extremely ill. I was hospitalised and ended up with Hepatitis A and jaundice. I lost so much weight and was so severely unwell, the authorities contemplated sending me home. Thankfully, I recovered and made it to the end of the course. During my time in India, I missed my family, and often thought of Rick and how life was treating him. There were no mobile phones, telecoms connections in Sierra Leone were poor, unreliable, and often unavailable. I had to write letters, which would take forever to get home. I learnt to cook Indian food and tried as best I could to maximize my time there. After we graduated, I flew to London to continue my studies.

SHATTERED DREAMS

I was picked up at the airport by my uncle and then very pregnant aunt, both of whom I had not spent much time with before nor knew very well, but we clicked instantly. They graciously opened their home to me and grafted me very willingly into their small but very beautifully bonded family. They had had a son who was 6 years old at the time, and my aunt's mother also lived with them. They lived in a 2-bedroom terrace house and had a very structured family life. I love order, so it was easy for me to find my place, and I felt so very welcomed.

I slept on a camp bed in the living room and spent endless nights watching TV, soaking in American Soaps that aired through the night in the UK. As we worked out the modalities of my residence and legalising my stay in the UK, my time with my uncle gave me ample time and space to get my head around the new culture. I experienced my first winter and had many falls in the snow much to my new family's amusement.

On cold winter mornings, my cousin Ryan would wake me up early on Saturday mornings to go build a snowman, much to my annoyance. I quickly realised that I really did not like being cold and felt very homesick on occasion. I contemplated totally changing my career to psychotherapy at that point. I have a natural knack for encouraging and counselling people and seriously toyed with setting up a stress management practice. However, I made enquiries, and when I understood the pathway for qualification, I was completely put off. In essence, it will take some seven years for the qualifying process to complete. In the UK, psychotherapy comes under the mental health sciences, and it is important to the governing bodies that practitioners are highly trained. After exploring my options, I decided that it was better to stick with IT as it was familiar to me, and I had already got two certifications.

I found a church family locally and attended fellowship regularly. I spent my time mostly preparing myself mentally for my next steps. I read a lot and rested especially as I had been so unwell in India and also knowing that busy days were just around the corner as I actively looked for a job.

One crisp and sunny morning in January as I was in the living room with my aunt, who was so due in a few weeks, and my grandma—her mother, we noticed a car going up and down our very short road. It went back and forth a few times, and it was evident to us that someone was either lost or looking for a particular house number, so it roused our suspicion. Suddenly, the car stopped in front of our house, and I ran to the window. Out stepped Rick! I thought my eyes were going to fall out of my head. I screamed so loudly that I am sure a dead person would have been jolted back to life. I ran to the front door, flung it open and jumped on Rick, spontaneously kissing his face severally.

"Oh my God!" Janet exclaimed.

"Had you told your aunt about him?" Rosa interjected.

"Interestingly, oh, by the way, we need a refill of this

lemonade.... Interestingly, just that morning, my aunt and grandma had been having that conversation with me. Prodding me about boys and my boyfriend."

It all happened when in a routine medical examination after my arrival from India when the doctor asked if I had had a smear and I responded "no."

He then responded, "Then, I will need to book you for one."

I turned up for my smear, and just before he proceeded, he asked, "Are you sexually active?"

I responded, "No."

He came out of the examining room and said to my uncle who had accompanied me to the appointment, "She is a virgin. She needs to start getting them done when she becomes sexually active." My uncle was startled and smiled as he thanked the doctor before we left.

The walk back home was quite awkward. We both said nothing, but he certainly would have told my aunt who used the information as the basis of the conversation we were having that morning. Her perspective was that it would be nice to have some "experience" and "exposure."

Rick carried me into the house as I was still hung on his neck. We settled down in the living room, and I offered him a drink. My aunt and grandma said their hellos and disappeared upstairs, eavesdropping for sure. All off a sudden, Rick went down on his knees and hung his head as he reached out to me for a hug.

I joined him on the floor, and as best he could, he tucked his face in my neck and held me reasonably tightly. "I am sorry Avril." he whispered as his voice cracked.

I jerked back, trying to catch a glimpse of his eye. Still on my knees, I sat back a bit, resting on my heels still holding his hands. "Rick, talk to me. What's going on? I haven't seen you in forever. So happy to be sharing this moment with you. Now you are crying?"

He looked up at me, and with tears in his eyes, he said, "Chica's pregnant."

I was stunned. Retorting in unbelief, "But not with your baby, surely Rick? Is it?"

He couldn't look at me. "Avril I am so sorry." He muttered as if he was losing his breath.

I broke down and wept bitterly. We held each other and cried. Again, the sense of betrayal and inexplicable loss I felt on losing Leo was rekindled. "Why Rick, what happened?" I asked stupidly.

Not a word more came from his lips! You could cut through the silence with a knife.

I was absolutely heartbroken. Rick apologised profusely after we had both stopped crying. Then he said "I really want us to be in touch. I miss you, and I need you in my life. I love you, and I don't want to lose you."

I said to him "I do not think that is a good idea. I am in a new season of my life, and there are new opportunities before me. I need to focus on what the future holds. All the while I was in India, I came to a realisation that I could love again and took a risk holding a flame in my heart for you. Now, you've blown it. I am sorry Rick. I am hurt right now, and I don't think it's such a good idea. At least not at this point. I will not be able to genuinely celebrate the birth of your child. You are very special to me, and I want to hold onto the beautiful memories we made in Freetown."

He tried to explain to me that the pregnancy was

unplanned and things were really not working for him and Chica as he had aforementioned, but there was too much confusion in my brain to appreciate or to process what he was saying.

Rick got up as if he had been hit by a big lorry, gave me a lingering hug, and sluggishly made his way to the door. As soon as I closed the door, I fell to my knees, and I burst into tears. My aunt and Grandma came downstairs and urged me to join them in the living room.

"See why I am so happy I did not sleep with Rick?" I said. "This is the problem. Men can't just keep their trousers zipped! Imagine Rick convincing me things were over between him and Chica while we were in Freetown, and the next minute crying like a baby because he had 'accidentally' impregnated her?"

"Dry your eyes girl." my grandma said firmly and authoritatively. "Your prince shall soon show up. Love is not supposed to make you cry so much."

My tears dried up alright, but there was an open wound in my heart. I had questions, and I missed my dad. I just longed to have a heart to heart with him.

I felt homesick, and if there was a way to go home for at least a long weekend, I would have. Loneliness in the midst of a family started creeping into my heart from time to time. For the most part, I was very happy, and again emotionally, I got better over time.

Things were still financially rough for the family back in Sierra Leone. Communication was via air mail letters. So it was quite normal to hear from the rest of the family once a month. One day as I was musing over my life and how God had perfectly juxtaposed the pieces beautifully, I began to recollect a story in the Bible of a young girl called Esther who was a Jew and had (against the odds) married a Persian king. There came a time when an evil agenda was conjured to wipe out the Jews, but Esther was strategically positioned to stand in the gap and petition the king for her people. Somehow it dawned on me similarly that being in the UK was just as timely for my family. I purposed to help my brothers as best I could and to support financially as much as was practical and doable.

A few months into my stay, I still had no job, and I desperately needed one in order to register for school and finance the furthering of my studies. I started contemplating an industry shift and even thought I might go back to Sierra Leone if a door doesn't open. I had moments of self-doubt and anxiety. So I began to pray and ask God if He really wanted me in the UK. I was away from my family, fair enough my uncle's house provided a loving and welcoming environment, but naturally my heart longed for home and my nuclear family.

One day after I had applied to the Home Office to be eligible to work and study in the UK, I had a dream. Usually, the application procedure back then took about three to six months on average to get approved. However, two weeks after my application, I had a dream that the postman brought my passport, and my residence application was approved. I woke up that morning, and surprise, surprise, the postman had delivered my passport. The following night, I had another dream that the roof of the house flew off and blessings fell on me from the sky. So much was the outpouring from Heaven that I literally had no room to contain it. I took these dreams as a sign that God wanted me in the UK, and He was going to prosper me in London. Especially that my residence had been approved so swiftly.

Soon after the arrival of my passport, I increased my aggression in looking for a job. I responded to a vacancy and applied to a college as a preliminary year lecturer and got the role the following month. It was so empowering that my plans were falling in place so beautifully. I enrolled in University and started pursing the completion of my degree course in IT. I continued to increase my knowledge of the country both in culture and geographically. I made new friends, and I finally settled in. London slowly became my new home, and I adapted to the way of life effortlessly.

In a few months after the start of my new job, I found an apartment and moved out of my uncle's place. My aunt had the baby, who happened to be a girl named after me, which delighted me no end! I bonded with her as if she was mine and purposed to spoil her as much as was humanly possible, so even though I had moved out of my uncle's house, I visited often, even babysitting on occasion.

After I started living on my own, it started a season of great loneliness. Never before had I lived on my own. Even though I was excited about being alone for the first time in my life, the silence of living without human contact was deafening. I constantly invited friends over for meals and movie nights or simply just to hangout. If I had missed my family before, the emotions I experienced at this time took my life to whole new place. I would come home evening after evening to an empty house and just long to have a hug or share a conversation of how my day went.

I still had a lot of settling in to do at the new place. However, I took my time to make it my castle. I had flat-packed cupboards, chest of drawers, bedroom and living room furniture to set up.

One day on my way to work, I had left home tastefully dressed. As I made my way to the bus stop that will connect me to the train that will get me to the office, perfectly made up, with a nice, fruity summer perfume and tastefully dressed—bag and shoes coordinated. As I walked to the bus stop, I heard "Avril?" very softly and almost as if the caller had a question. He called out again, and I saw a very familiar face. *I have definitely seen this person before*, I thought.

"Akpon! Oh, my days! It's been forever." I blurted as the fullness of the memory came back to me. I had met Akpon in a chance meeting with his older brother years ago at a Christian event.

"My goodness! You haven't aged a day. Avril, you look so good!" He delightfully exclaimed. We chatted a while as he walked me to the bus stop. We got talking and realised we lived in the same neighbourhood literally across a green from each other. I told him to come by and visit after work as I had to rush off.

Sure enough, after work, he was there waiting for me at the bus stop. I walked him to my place, got some dinner for us both, and we sat down and talked late into the night. It was like we knew each other all our lives. I complained about the flat-packed furniture that had to be set up, and Akpon willingly volunteered to help, seeing that he was then unemployed. I was in utter disbelief and thought, *this guy is so nice*. I asked him if he wanted to be paid, and he would have none of it. I was overwhelmed by his generosity with his time and energy. I naively gave him a set of keys, and he agreed to turn up every day and worked all day.

He made so much progress that I promised him that if he completed all that needed to be done at the end of the next week, I will cook him dinner. True to his estimation, the work of setting up my furniture was completed, so true to my word, I made my way home early from work that Friday, went grocery shopping, and laid out a feast. We sat grazing over canapés, through a very hearty main meal unto a very unforgiving dessert. We chatted effortlessly and looked up, suddenly it was 3am. We both could not believe how time had flown by.

My newfound friend filled my need for companionship. He visited me daily after work and sharing my dinner became a regular occurrence. Very quickly, he became my only and best friend. We spoke about any and everything. I found it strange that this seemingly perfect guy was not on speaking terms with his own mother and clearly carried a lot of bitterness about his father being absent while he and his brother were raised single-handedly by their mother. He also told me he had a girlfriend in Africa with whom he has decided to end his relationship with as they had drifted apart. Our friendship continued, and somehow, probably due to my own lonesomeness and homesickness, I found myself becoming increasingly emotionally attached to this guy even though initially I had not found him attractive nor 'husband material' by my estimation.

One day, I asked him to accompany me to a friend, Phil's house. Phil had travelled and had asked me to go to his house daily to feed his cat and water the house plants. When we arrived at Phil's place, Akpon said, "Avril, I really need to talk to you."

"Go on, I am listening," I said as I walked around looking for the cat.

"No," he said rather irritated. "I need your full and undivided attention. You always do so many things at the same time. I need to tell you something. This is really important, and you can't be feeding a cat or doing whatever when I need to talk. This is super important."

"Okay," I said as I strutted across the room hugging and stroking the cat. Akpon found a spot to sit, and I could see that he had somehow gone into deep thought.

The silence that followed was deafening, punctuated intermittently by his nervous breathing. I went on to feed the cat, open the windows to let some fresh air in, and watered the plants. So when I was done, I sat down to have to this all important conversation. "Avril. I have loved you since the moment I met you. You have provided me friendship and being a confidant. I have come to love you so deeply I would like to take our friendship a step further. Will you be my girlfriend? When I have my breakthrough, I will want you to be my wife."

I paused with a million things running through my head. Akpon was jobless and homeless. He lived with a friend of his, and apart from the fact that we had great rapport and that we were both practising Christians, we had nothing else in common. My emotions were all over the place.

Sure, we were great friends, and he was somewhat dependable but surely not someone I saw as the man with whom I will want to spend my life! His proposal had come to me totally unexpectedly. In response I said, "I am travelling to Africa for a break shortly. Please let me think it over then, and I will let you know my thoughts when I get back."

Before I could finish my sentence, Akpon got up and started to kiss me. I did not resist. I suppose a part of me had greatly softened toward him too. We kissed passionately, and I KNEW our relationship had changed.

Actually in retrospect, one day while I was at work, I took ill and came down with the flu. I had been nursing a cold for a few days, and it escalated to a full-blown flu. I decided to leave work early and go home. I called Akpon and told him I will make it home as I was just not in a fit state to spend the day working. By the time I got home, he had gone shopping and cooked me some soup, taken my dirty laundry to the laundrette, and ironed my clothes—just so that I could spend the weekend in bed and get better. I was so blown away by his seeming kindness, I remember thinking for myself, *my world, what a good man.*

Suddenly, I saw qualities of selflessness that I desired in a husband. Such a darling. He was keen to move things forward and somehow had marriage on his mind, so he capitalized on my admiration for his selflessness and told me, "My wife is going to be the happiest woman ever. I would spoil her to bits."

However, the fact that it was clear to me that he was not financially or seemingly emotionally ready for marriage, still played at the back of my mind, so I wanted time to think things over and more importantly, talk over with him about his plans and goals for his life since he lacked a sense of direction and conviction of who he was and where he was going.

I did go on holiday, only to come back and find out that our relationship status had been publicised to our peer group and social circle. I felt really weird because while I was away, I felt I wanted to discuss my concerns before moving forward. Nonetheless, I accepted our new position in each other's lives (as dating exclusively) without questions and life moved on.

Our relationship was far from perfect. I had high expectations, and we were clearly not on par as far as our past was concerned. We had bitter arguments and broke up several times. The chasm of the differences we had seemed to get wider and wider. I found myself working really hard to make things work. Akpon felt continually misunderstood and used every emotional manipulation available to humankind to get what he wanted.

It was a regular practice for me to watch soaps. Due to work and study commitments, I would record the individual episodes of the soaps I loved to watch and put together an omnibus, which I will watch on a Friday or Saturday night. One Friday, Akpon turned up and requested he watch another programme. We went back and forth as I really wanted to watch my recordings. I conceded, going to cook instead. After all, my programs were recorded, so I could watch them at a later time. While in the kitchen, I arrange my ingredients and prepared myself to get lost in my 'office' as I even referred to my kitchen back then. I raised the volume of the radio as one Tina Turner number blasted into the air waves after another. I slid across the floor from one end to the other as I mimed the words of the songs. All of a sudden, Akpon rushed into the kitchen and shouted, "What the hell do you think you are doing? What kind of songs are these anyway?" I was so stunned that I was rendered speechless. He proceeded to push the radio on to the floor, smashing it. Again, he stormed out of the house as he screamed, "It is over."

I was left speechless and confused. I curled up into a ball and cried so hard. I tried calling him to make sense of what had just happened, but he refused to pick up. I lost the desire to cook. I put the things back in the fridge, cleaned up the pieces of my broken radio, and went to bed. The following day, I met up with Akpon who apologised profusely and said he felt provoked by the songs on the radio.

"You don't say," Rosa interrupted. "This is madness on a different level."

To say I found this disturbing is an understatement, but as usual he blamed the Devil. I forgave him, got on with life, and brushed it off as a dip in the road. These angry outbursts continued, and I was constantly left mesmerized by how one person can carry so much anger. Akpon was constantly angry about one thing or the other. However, he always had a way of explaining away his bad behaviour, so I learnt to live with it especially because he promised that he realised he needed to do something about it and promised to go to anger management and seek spiritual deliverance.

Our makeup sessions were passionate, and he knew how and where to touch me. Just kissing and fondling would often lead me to an orgasm—something I had not experience with any other man. So in spite of the volatile nature of our relationship, there was an unhealthy emotional entanglement.

Now living on my own, even though in a relationship, I missed home and my family. After numerous discussions, it was decided that one of my brothers will join me for company. So Brian, after year 9, flew into the UK to join me. What a joyous and memorable day that was. I went to the airport hours before the plane was due to land, and in my excitement, I could not eat. When Brian came through the doors, I screamed, ran past people, and jumped on him. He almost fell over. My joy was uncontainable. Suddenly, my life changed. We had little sleep in the days that followed. The bond between Brian and I deepened. He easily became my closest sibling. We confided and shared our joys, fears, and dreams. Brian naturally has a quiet disposition, so there was never a confrontation between him and Akpon. All he did was urge me to pray because he was uneasy about a lot of things he saw. I felt in many ways so very responsible to ensure Brian was okay, happy, fed, clothed, sheltered, and educated. My love and care for Brian was like that of a dependent child. I effectively became his mum. We did everything together. Brian's being in London took the sharpness of the pain of detachment from the family and loneliness I felt. That season is forever etched in my heart with so many beautiful memories.

Things back in Sierra Leone seemed to descend into a downward spiral. The government had been overthrown in a military coup. There was a lot of tension in Sierra Leone. Basic amenities were unavailable, and the citizens were really struggling to live. Telecom connectivity was patchy and unreliable. Within these constraints, Brian and I kept in touch with our parents. Whenever our mum or dad could call, they did. They were much happier that Brian was with me and that I had found someone to date. I kept my relationship woes from them as I did expect things will get better with time.

I had a distinct feeling that something was not right with my dad. I started having recurrent dreams of him in a coffin, and it left me very unsettled. I would often wake up covered in a cold sweat and frantically called home to check if my dad was ok. He was diabetic, and sometimes, we had to get his medication sent all the way from the UK. I prayed about those dreams as best I could, but the dreams became frequent and troubling.

One day Akpon, Brian and I came back from a shopping trip, and I just felt really tired. I decided to take a brief afternoon nap. I had the most interesting experience. I wasn't fully asleep, yet I wasn't awake enough to get up and move around. To anyone looking at me, I appeared to be asleep. However, I could hear everything that was going on around me. Somehow, I had a very strange dream. I dreamt I was in a church meeting and the late Benson Idahosa (a charismatic Pentecostal preacher who ignited the fire of Pentecostalism in Africa) was hosting a meeting.

He called me out from the crowd and said, "Gather strength. Something will soon happen that will shake you to your core and the foundations of your life. Never forget that God has always got you."

I left the meeting (still dreaming) and found myself at age 11 back in the house where we lived. Suddenly, I heard one word: "look." I turned around and saw numerous angels standing shoulder to shoulder. All of a sudden, I saw the lorry enter the house that we lived in. I then heard the same voice again saying, "If I could deliver your dad when he did not know me, how much more now?"

I woke up from the trance-like experience. I called Akpon and Brian and told them what I had just experienced. Brian suggested I call our pastor. I did, and he prayed with me. I had the urge to call home and check on my dad. I called the next day. My dad passed that night!

I made a phone call, and the call was picked up by Jesse. When I asked, "How is dad? Is everything alright? I am troubled because I have been having some strange dreams."

He simply dropped the phone. Strangely this continued with every call I made in the next 3 days. I relented, thinking it was a usual problem with connectivity.

Finally, about 5 days after the trance, I was called by a woman who Akpon had introduced to me as a mother figure. She told me she had a problem with Akpon and wanted to discuss it with me. She sounded really distressed and urged me to get to her house as soon as I possibly could. She lived within a stone's throw of where I lived. I did not even have a change of clothes.

I simply put a jacket on and walked to her house. Upon entering the house, I was shocked to see all the members of a choir I was part of. I thought to myself that whatever this problem was that Akpon had with this woman, must be very serious. She asked me to sit down. I found a chair and without beating about the bush she blurted out, "Your dad passed away on the 20th." I felt a chill right down my spine, and I wasn't sure I heard right, so I asked her to repeat what she had just said. She said very pointedly but with as much sensitivity that she could conjure up at that moment. She looked at me in my eyes, apologised firstly, and then said, "Darling your father died."

I felt the room spinning, and I screamed loudly, I fell down on the floor and cried out loudly. I got up and try to strangle this woman. The pain of separation I felt in that moment took years to heal. I became totally hysterical. I ran out of the house on to the main road, screaming. As many people as could run after me, but being a former athlete, no one could catch me. I ran into oncoming traffic, heading nowhere, dodging cars in my path. I ran until there was no strength left in me, and I just fell down on the footpath of the main road. I was picked up and taken back to the lady's house—physically exhausted and emotionally broken.

As I returned, I saw my brother on the balcony weeping uncontrollably. The lady asked me to stay with her the night. I did not sleep a wink. The next day, I called home and my mum picked up the phone. As soon as I said hello, we both started crying. There were no words. Just tears.

I purposed to go home and bury my beloved father. I felt a dark cloud looming over me. I sank into a depression. In the midst of it all, I remembered my dreams and gathered strength. I asked God for fortitude, and He gave it. I felt like I was upheld by angels. There was such a very real and present sense of comfort.

I turned up in Freetown and was picked up by Joe. The trip home was solemn laced with intermittent crying. When I saw Mum, she had suddenly lost a lot of weight, and her grief was indescribable. In the Sierra Leonean tradition, in the event of a funeral, the extended family virtually moves in from the day someone passes to the day they are buried. This time is called "The Sitting." Friends and sympathizers will continually stream to the house to support, encourage, and uphold the grieving family.

A few days after I landed in Freetown, I was taken to go view my father's corpse. We drove to the mortuary, and

I was feeling very weak (due to the excessive crying and the fact that I had not been eating). At some point on the journey, I began to debate with myself if this was a good idea. We arrived at the morgue after what seemed like an eternity and went through the formalities to view my beloved father's corpse. We were taken into a room where his mortal remains were wheeled out. As soon as I saw him with cotton wool in his nostrils and ears, a new wave of reality hit me that indeed Daddy was no longer with us, and I fainted.

I recovered, surrounded by my aunties and the workers at the mortuary, went back home, and sat out the days next to my mum until the dark day when daddy was buried. 20 years on, the memories of that day still brings tears to my eyes. When we came back from the cemetery, there was such a sense of emptiness. I decided to call Akpon. I left the crowd who were congregated in the repast we had at the house and went upstairs. I dialled Akpon, and he answered promptly.

"How was it, Avril?" He asked sympathetically.

"My God Akpon, the whole day is such a blur. Daddy rests in the bosom of Christ, so I am at peace I will see him again. The parting though. The parting is so very painful."

Our conversation was interrupted with my outbursts of crying. "Akpon. I am ready to get married. I cannot bear to lose another person in my life."

"Are you sure Avril"? He asked excitedly.

"I am serious," I replied.

"Well plan it all on your return, and I will make sure I show up" He said with his usual tongue-in-cheek humour.

Marriage

The days of traditional mourning ended, and I returned to the UK with such an open wound in my soul. There were days that there was so much grief in my heart, I could not put the pain into words. It is interesting how people seemingly get on with life after the formal laying to rest or cremation of someone who has passed. Truly, only the heart that loves knows the sorrow and pain of parting.

I started making plans to get married even though I was not formerly engaged. Akpon had hinted on asking me so many times, but because our relationship was so turbulent, I just couldn't 'go there.' So many times before, I had resolved that I will not be able to marry Akpon—there were too many rough edges, but there was a vulnerability about him in spite of his public image as a 'hard nut to crack' that made me feel that I could help and maybe change him. That was a dangerous assumption, but naïvely, I thought suddenly that in the face of my father's death, somehow everything will miraculously be perfect.

I began to put wedding plans in place, and now in retrospect, I wonder what I was thinking. Akpon did not seem remotely interested in his own wedding plans. His favourite phrase was, "I don't have money, so you just organise everything." I somehow convinced myself that men are not that interested in weddings, and I got on with my plans. We, well I, set a date. I then reminded Akpon that even though he had asked me to marry him informally in the past, we were not officially engaged. So he took me to the jewellers to purchase a ring.

He asked me to pick out the ring of my choice, and

I felt that the world was my oyster. I found a nice diamond clustered gold ring. He then turned to me and said, "Darling, can you please loan me the money? I promise to pay you back."

My dear friends, to this day, I am waiting to be paid back. He took the ring and said he will organise a romantic surprise proposal. Our wedding was fast approaching. He asked me out to dinner one night and asked me to get very nicely dressed as it was a special night. I got my best dress, and we went on the bus (as neither of us had a car at the time), and the bus was cheaper that taking the train.

It took us forever to go the mystery restaurant, which turned out to be a Chinese restaurant in Piccadilly Circus in Central London that we had been to before. I was NOT impressed at all, but I hoped that the night will unfold some pleasant surprises. Finally, just as we ordered our dessert, he took the ring out of his pocket and opened the box.

I was so horrified that he did not kneel down to ask me properly. I had tears in my eyes and asked sadly, "Akpon, can't you at least ask me properly?"

He said, "Avril, Africans do not kneel down in an engagement. It is not within the culture. Are you going to take the ring or are you going to sit there looking at it?"

I took the ring and placed it on my finger. I was so sad in my heart. Dessert was served, and we ate quietly. As I ate, I kept thinking *what just happened?* Thankfully, he paid. We left and returned home. I was surprised the next morning when I had a flood of calls from our mutual friends congratulating me on our engagement. Again, he had announced it to the world.

Our wedding was 2 months away, and there was still

so much left undone. I rallied my friends around, and we approach the last leg of the wedding preparations like a project our lives depended on. Mum was travelling to be at my wedding and to give herself a much needed break in the aftermath of my dad's death. Her imminent arrival created such an excitement in my heart. As the wedding grew closer, I increasingly became uneasy about the decision to marry. Everything that had happened in our relationship, the angry outbursts, the way the engagement happened, and the fact that I had paid for my own engagement ring, made me apprehensive about what the future might hold. A couple of weeks before the wedding, I called a cousin of mine and asked that we meet for lunch.

When we met up, I explained to her how I was feeling and that I wanted to call off the wedding. The invites had been sent out, the cake ordered, and my dress was ready, but my heart felt very uncertain. I just did not want to do it. My cousin convinced me that I was having cold feet, and it is too late to walk away from the whole thing. That it was perfectly normal to feel nervous because it was such a significant move in someone's life that it poses a scare to some people. I left the lunch date convinced that I was having cold feet and that all will be okay.

On the morning of the wedding, one of the girls I had chosen to be a bridesmaid, who happened to be Akpon's adopted sister, phoned me to tell me that she did not like the colour theme I had chosen, and as such, she was no longer willing to be my bridesmaid. I could not believe my ears. I decided that level of betrayal would not deter me from having a great day. I went over to one of my aunt's house to get dressed. Another uncle of mine, his wife—my aunt, and one of my grandparents was there, too. My brother Brian came along. My mum had encountered several difficulties in making it to the wedding and was finally on her way to London on the day of my wedding.

A few minutes after arriving at my aunt's place, we had a call from my cousin who had gone to pick Mum up at the airport. The plane had been delayed from Freetown; therefore, they were unable to make the connection in Brussels. It dawned on me that after all the preparations, my mum was not going to make it to the wedding ceremony. It was like cryptic messages of all creation crying out, "Don't do it!"

The day went on without a hitch. I got my hair done, got dressed, and got in the waiting limo, and arrived at church a few mins late—as is traditional of brides. I walked down the aisle to a song, and I can still vividly recollect in my thoughts. There was so much expectation in my heart. I had kept my virginity and was so excited about finally giving myself sexually as I felt this is the best gift that I could give my husband. I was hoping that in the eyes of my husband to be I was the most beautiful girl he had seen and that finally beyond my physical looks, he could see the treasures that lay within me and would do his best to be the best husband.

Not a single one of his family members attended the wedding. His father was estranged from him, but his mother and brother with whom he had grown up were reluctant to apply for a visa in the assumption that they would be refused. He promised me he had informed a number of his extended family, but no one of his blood relatives were there. However, a number of his friends made it to the wedding.

The service went smoothly. We made our vows, shared

our first kiss as husband and wife, signed the register, and headed on to a very well organised, simple, and beautiful reception ceremony. The speeches were heartfelt, the food tasty, and the music on point. However, when it was time for the first dance, Akpon decided he did not want to dance. It took persuasions from my uncles that he should at least dance on his own wedding day. He reluctantly conceded, and finally, we had our first dance. The embarrassment was so intense. I felt like disappearing

My mum arrived during the reception and was welcomed very warmly. I went up to hug my mum, and she was so emotional. As she held me, she whispered, "Baby girl, you look so beautiful. I wish Daddy was here."

We both wiped tears from each other's eyes. The reception went on as planned and the after party was delightful and memorable. Akpon however, refused to dance. He had to be urged and coerced on to the dance floor by my uncles several times. His excuse was that he did not like the music.

We retired to the place we had secured to be our marital home. This was an apartment that a friend of ours owned. He was living there, but life's circumstances moved him out to Wales, so for the 3 months he would be away, he graciously allowed us to start married life there. We went off to Brighton for a few days for honeymoon. Married life started in earnest. Some of Akpon's friends had reservations about the success of our marriage. Once when I walked into the apartment, I overheard a very uncomplimentary telephone conversation about me Akpon was having with a friend of his. I waited until the conversation was over and confronted him about it. "Why on earth do you listen in on my telephone calls?" he retorted.

I went on to explain that I had not purposely eavesdropped his conversation. I just happened to walk in and heard him talking. He was livid!

He picked up the phone, dialled the person again, and told them I had eavesdropped. He went on to affirm his commitment to their friendship. I felt such a sense of betrayal, and it made me wonder if I could ever trust my own husband.

My mum had sent some food over, and I decided to freeze it and get us to eat it at another time as I had seasoned some chicken for dinner that night. I went on to prepare a hearty meal and invited him to the table. When he came over and realised I had cooked, " . . . just chicken, potatoes and vegetables," he lost it.

"Where is the African food that Mum sent?" he screamed.

"I decided we could have that another day because I had seasoned this chicken prior to her food arriving." He got up, picked up his jacket, and stormed out of the house.

Back then, I did not own a mobile phone, so I had no idea where he had gone nor could I reach him. Akpon stayed out all night. We had only been married a week. I called Mum to explain what had happened.

She was so disheartened, she muttered, "Hmm, I have reservations for the success of this marriage. What is his problem? Tell me my princess, what kind of relationship did you guys have?"

I could hardly speak. She consoled me as best she could, and we ended our call. Early the next morning, Akpon came back. He went on his knees and apologised profusely. He said he was really upset and just sat by the roadside all night. I chose to forgive him even though I know he did not sit outside on the pavement all night. We swept the matter under the carpet and moved on. Things settled somewhat.

Mum stayed for 6 months after the wedding and was so thankful that I was married. In her estimation, the love my husband would shower me with would help with the grieving process of Dad's passing, and as she had been very happily married herself, she wished the same for me plus more. My mum was at peace that she could leave and go settle things back in Sierra Leone. Dad had passed on so suddenly that he had not left a will, and things needed to be put in place properly. Mum also was in a much better place emotionally and was prepared to start rebuilding her life as a widow.

A Dark Corridor

After mum left, we found an apartment through a housing association. What was deeply troubling to me at this time was that Akpon had a really bad credit record, so everything we needed on credit became my responsibility. Akpon was unemployed when we met and took on a job as a security guard initially from which he was fired. He promised to look for and secure work to no avail, so I became the primary bread winner. I paid the rent, bought groceries, clothed him, fed him. It was like having a grown child. This too created pressure in my mind and was constantly a source of friction. Anyway, 6 months into our marriage, Mum left. A week after she left, we were in the living room watching a little 14-inch TV that was the only TV we had. When the programme we were watching finished, we both wanted to watch two different things. We started to have a tug of war with the remote control. It was all very humorous, and then, Akpon left for the loo.

When he came back, I had tuned to the programme I desired to watch and hid the remote under the cushion I sat on. He looked everywhere for it frantically while my show continued. As time went on, he became more and more agitated and annoyed. Finally, he found the remote and went into a total tirade that dissolved into a violent outburst. It was so reminiscent of the historic incident in my apartment. He folded me over on the couch and sat on me, repeating over and over, "How does that feel? How dare you hide the remote? What does that feel like?" I was struggling to breathe when he finally got off me.

He then went around the apartment, breaking things. He took some of our wedding presents and smashed them into pieces. I ran into a corner and curled up like a little child as I sobbed uncontrollably. When the wave of anger subsided, he took a broom and cleaned up the debris as he wept blaming the devil.

He walked over to me and kissed me gently with tears in his eyes. "Avril, I promise I am going to get help. This anger is out of control. Please sweetie do not mention this to anyone. I will go to town tomorrow and replace some of the broken things." Akpon wept so bitterly, I felt sorry for him.

As time went on, I slowly began to purchase the basic furnishings we needed for the apartment as I began to create my little castle in that home. As I shopped excitedly month after month, Akpon did not lift a finger to help with putting flat-packed furnishing together. He claimed he was not a DIY enthusiast, and he would rather not damage things while trying to put them together. My brother often had to spend weekends with us, helping me furnish my marital home. I purposed I was going to demonstrably love my husband until he came to a realisation of what marriage was all about and how selfless one needs to be as a spouse. So I purposely refused to react negatively to most things he threw my way.

As you guys know, we hail from different cultures, background, and life experiences. There were days when I would have lovingly prepared a meal. He would get home, only to yell at me, and toss the food in the bin or just walk away from the table. Now you guys know, your girl can hold it down in the kitchen, so it's not like the food was inedible. However, to make life hell for me, he constantly criticized my cooking.

I decided to raise my game. Whenever he would return home from being out, I would take off his shoes, wash his feet, and massage them. Just in a bid to soften his disposition toward me. One day while I was at work, he called me as asked when I'd be home as he wanted to discuss something with me. When I walked in, he was stoically sat in one of the arm chairs. There was so much tension in the room. As I sat down, he blurted out, "Avril, I think I have made a mistake!"

I was stunned.

Not fully understanding what he meant, I asked, "What have you done?"

"I married you," he responded. "I should never have done it."

"So why do you feel it's a mistake? Don't you love me? What's really bugging you, Akpon?" I asked as I got up and walked closer to him. I sat on the arm of the chair and put my hand on his arm.

"I feel trapped. We are two different creatures. I simply do not want to be married to you anymore."

I turned to him and said, "We have to work this out. We have just had a big wedding and less than a year later, you are telling me you want out? I did not intend to waste all those people's time, and I can understand that you did not grow up in a traditional family setting, but please don't throw in the towel so early. I made my vows for better or worse, so baby, we are going to stick this out till death do us part. I meant those vows. What is wrong with you?"

He looked at me completely emotionless, shook his head, got up, and walked away.

He went to the bathroom, had a shower, got dressed, and went out without saying where he was going. This episode started a tradition that broke the rule of accountability. When we woke up the next morning, I asked him where he has been. He looked at me and said, "Don't you ever ask me about my movements, I am not a child. I do not have to tell you or anyone where I am going. As a matter of fact, I have a friend who has decided to cook for me now and again, so from time to time, I will go by her place to grab dinner."

I was suddenly the other woman in my own marriage, and it did not get better. On one occasion when we were having sex, Akpon consistently screamed out the name of one of his exes. I began to recoil from being intimate. There were occasions when if he wanted intimacy, he would force intimacy whether I was in the mood or not. He would tear off my nightdress and force himself on me without foreplay. On a few occasions in the aftermath of lovemaking, I could not walk straight. Not only was he rough with me in bed, on occasion, if we had an argument, and I was within arm's length, I might land myself a slap.

The physical abuse was compounded with mental and verbal abuse. I longed to receive compliments, but all I got was criticism. He complained about the size of my boobs, the size of my waist, my skin complexion, my height, and just about everything he could call out. He wanted out of our marriage so badly that he projected bad behaviour constantly. I remember once when I was getting dressed, he looked at me and said, "You have the face of an angel but the body of a monkey." On another occasion, he said, "You are so skinny, I am sure people think you have AIDS."

These events sent me into a very dark place, and I could not stop grieving for my dad. Once I was sat on the toilet seat sobbing, he heard me from outside the toilet, opened the door, and asked, "why are you crying?"

"I miss my dad so much," I replied.

He then said, "When would this idolatry in your heart end? The man is gone. His era has ended. Why can't you move on? Please, I do not want you practising idolatry in our home! Please don't let me ever find you crying and the reason you are crying is because of your father." He then stepped out and closed the door.

I decided that as a Christian, I was not going to end my marriage without a fight. At this point, we had been married for about 2 years. I had not mentioned a single word to any of my family members, hoping that whatever had possessed Akpon to be such a horrible person would leave him, and we will be fine. I tried to interject moment of happiness and to create an atmosphere that will nurture loving feelings, but all my efforts were of no effect. I would buy sexy clothes and try to entice him.

I organised for us to have romantic dinners, organised weekends away, movie dates, etc.

I prayed constantly. After all, I had gone according to the Good Book. I had kept myself for marriage. I had, as best I could, been a good wife. I had tried to keep a good clean home and avoided arguments as much as possible. I decided as a last resort that maybe, just maybe if I have a baby, I will win this man over. On a few occasions, I brought up the subject, and it sent Akpon into a very strange place. I found this interesting because while we were dating, we had discussed how many kids we would love to have, the genders we wanted, and even names.

Anyway, I decided to get off my contraception to try for a child. Apart from the desire to fix things, I desperately longed to be a mother. In the 3rd month of trying, I found out I was pregnant. I remember standing in front of the mirror in the bathroom, gently caressing my belly and being full of nothing pure joy and gratitude to God that he has found me worthy of being a mother. There and then, I promised my unborn child that I will be the best mum in the world and just fantasised on what the future holds.

After what seemed like an eternity, I emerged from the bathroom and phoned my GP to confirm the home pregnancy test I had done. I was given a prompt appointment. The doctor confirmed that I had a bun in the oven and gave me a prescription for the vitamins I should take for the first three months. I kept the pregnancy a secret until I was 3 months along. I was just too scared to say anything. Finally, my body started to change, and I had to tell Akpon he was going to be a dad. I remember that Saturday morning as if it was yesterday. I gingerly walked up to Akpon while he was in the kitchen, and as nervous as a leaf, I stuttered that I had missed my period.

He flew into such a rage I ran into the bathroom and locked myself in there. He kept pounding the door while screaming, "Why are you trying to trap me in this marriage?" He was furious and enraged.

After his temper subsided, he left the house. After a few hours, he came back with a couple of his friends. The people tried 'talking some sense' to my head as to whether it was the wisest thing to keep the baby seeing that things are just not working between us.

I looked at Akpon squarely in the eyes and said, "If this baby was on a jar on a table, you could knock it over and break the jar, but so long as he or she is inside me, it is going to grow to term and be given a chance at life."

He used my determination to keep the baby, as an example to his friends that I was stubborn and that's why our marriage was in such a mess. The pregnancy was rough, and I was very unwell coupled with the fact that Akpon totally abandoned me emotionally. He provided absolutely no support whatsoever.

My brother Brian took a gap year from university to give me support. To this day, I cannot thank him enough for that. He was there to rub my back, follow me to my scans, and just hang out with me on my down days. I was in and out of hospital as I bled right through the pregnancy. When I was six months along, I started having a strange discharge. A series of tests were done on me, and the doctors concluded I had contracted a sexually transmitted disease. Obviously as a pregnant woman, I could only have had it from one source. I confronted Akpon, and it became another argument that didn't solve anything.

My brother patiently supported me through the various seasons of the pregnancy, helped me with shopping for baby things, and even helped me with baby name selections. When the baby was full term due to an earlier detection of a small pelvis, I was scheduled for a caesarean section. I turned up at the hospital on the due date, and my baby, a healthy 7lbs 11oz bouncing baby boy who looked exactly like me, was delivered at 2:45 pm. When I held him, a fountain of love sprung up from my heart that over the years has grown to a stream, to a river, to a sea and is now as large as the ocean.

Akpon showed up at the hospital after a couple of days of me having the baby. He had an argument with me that I would not have a quickie with him on my hospital bed while there was a massive bandage across my stomach, and I was still bleeding from the delivery. I really did not know how or what he wanted, but he was not happy that now that the baby was out, I did not automatically respond to his advances. I was discharged after a week and went home to start life as a new mum. It was so tiring yet so very exciting. A few months after the baby was born, I had to go back to studying and to work as I only had 3 months maternity break on full pay. Through the upheavals of our frail marriage, I had taught Akpon to drive and had taught him computing like a child. At the time I had our son, I had already done my first year of a master's programme. I took a break while I was pregnant and had to go back into the second year four months after the delivery. Life became busy, exhausting, and I was very thinly stretched, but the joy in my heart was unquantifiable. My name was forever changed from Avril to Mama.

Our marriage continued to fail. Brian returned to university, and coincidentally and to my advantage, Jesse needed somewhere to live for a few months, so he asked if he could crash in our spare room. He moved in with us, and oh how he and our young son Adiel bonded was magical. Akpon extended the shacking of his responsibility to the baby and became even more detached after he was born. My expectation that a baby would bring us closer did the exact opposite. Akpon started going out for days at a time. The sheer embarrassment of not knowing where my husband was at on occasion was so overwhelming especially if people called the house and enquired of him. I would come up with one story after the other.

As things took a downward spiral, I sought counselling. I made an appointment with our pastor and had a 'no bars holding' session. I explained to our pastor how bleak things looked. The first thing he asked was, "Why did you marry when you has so many doubts?"

For the first time in three years, illumination came to me. I was finally able to reason and to understand my plight. Right out of my own reasoning, it occurred to me as I answered the pastor. "Pastor, I was looking for love after my dad passed away. I married my husband on a rebound, and I now realise it is the biggest mistake of my life."

The pastor listened keenly and decided that he would call Akpon for a series of counselling sessions. I was amazed at how Akpon freaked out on an invite to have counselling for the betterment of our marriage as we experienced a few nasty days. I was so desperate to not raise a child in hostility and indifference, so it was important to now open up to someone and seek help.

The date of our counselling arrived and surprise, surprise, Akpon agreed to drive with me to the pastor's office. We arrived, and the pastor asked him to shed light on his perspective of things. Without wasting time, he went straight to the point and said, "Pastor, I have made a mistake in marrying Avril. I have come to the unquestionable conclusion that I do not love her, I never did—at least not enough to go the distance in marriage. So the best thing is for us to break up."

The pastor urged him to try and work things out as now we had a son between us. He said he will see how things go. The session ended, and Akpon decided to go home alone. I drove home with Adiel and cried my eyes out. All of a sudden, it dawned on me that our marriage was not over, it never started. A few months into marriage when Akpon had asked me for an out, I should have honoured his request and released him.

When he got home, he asked for a formal separation so that he can think through things. I moved to the spare room, and Jesse started sleeping on the couch. I cried all night long. The last time that happened was when dad passed.

Akpon sat me down the next morning (probably from hearing me cry all night) and said he really wanted to step up to the plate and face his responsibility as a man in our home. He wanted to give this thing a try. I felt some light pierce my present darkness. Finally, my heart leapt at the possibility of the hope that our marriage could be saved. Before I could process what he was saying, he interjected my thoughts with his continuing statements. This was going to be on his terms, in his way, and in his time. I agreed.

He wanted a trial separation to 'find himself,' but his conjugal rights remained as we were very much married. He wanted time to grow whatever love he felt in our courtship days, and he wanted to take over the financial responsibility of the home. I breathed a sigh of relief. I was in total agreement even though I did not fully understand why he wanted us living totally separated lives under the same roof. Up until that point, I had been the primary bread winner (as Akpon just could not find and keep a job), and I found it emotionally and psychologically burdensome.

Whatever represented some respite to my current situation was just very welcome. He asked me to follow him to the housing office to hand over our apartment to him as the primary tenancy account holder. I joyously did. I did a monthly projection of our outgoings and handed him to provide guidance on the financial running of the home. I continued to give him IT lessons and urged him to get a job as an IT trainer for MS applications. I made him a CV and sent him into industry, connecting him to a few of my contacts. He was called for a couple of interviews, and one of the opportunities made him an offer. Akpon finally stepped on the corporate ladder. When he came home from the interview that offered him the job and I asked what the re-numeration was, he simply and very calmly told me to mind my business and that it wasn't important for my knowledge, seeing that I had agreed to a trial separation. To say that after the endless days of training and grooming I was left speechless is an understatement. However, I kept my lips sealed for the sake of peace.

Akpon's resolve to take responsibility and his desire to be the man of the house, a good husband and father, was very short lived. He started to complain about how much milk Adiel was having. He emphatically called me one day and established that I must cut back on his feeding and how would henceforth only buy what he felt was reasonable.

Akpon had put his physical abuse on hold while Jesse lived with us and he would often help me with babysitting. One day, he called Jesse and told him we had agreed that he must start paying rent for sleeping on our couch. Jesse was really perturbed by this decision that Akpon alleged was mutually arrived upon by us both. He told Akpon that he would rather move out. It was only a couple of months before his place would be ready, but he decided to move out and go stay with a friend. It was not until after Jesse moved out that I realised the dialogue had taken place.

Soon after Jesse moved out, I had to go take my final exam. I had almost quit the course on a few occasions when things had gotten really rough. Somehow, on the morning of my exam, Akpon and I had a major argument. He got up and decided that he will not look after our son while I needed to go take my exam. I placed our son in his car seat and walked out. As I headed for the car, Akpon shouted, "You will bury your child when you return because I am going to leave him to die. I am not going to touch him. I am going to take him right into the middle of the road!"

I turned up to take my exam, and I must have looked a right state. Everyone was asking why my eyes were so blood shot. I went to the bathroom, and I realised I must have been grieved inexplicably at what happened in the morning. I had never seen my own countenance like that. I went into the exam and gave it my best shot.

I came from the exam, and of course, he had done nothing untoward to Adiel. A few weeks later, the physical violence in the marriage started again. On occasion if he desired intimacy and I wasn't in the mood, he will rip off my night dress and force himself on me. We had been seeing the pastor, and it never ceased to amaze me that Akpon did not act on a single suggestion for restoration that that pastor gave us. Akpon was a law unto himself. I do not know whether his inability to be open to corrected or be accountable had anything to do with the fact that his father left them when he was only 2 years old, and he virtually raised himself as his mum worked every hour that God sent to look after them or whether he was just arrogant, egotistical, and conceited.

Once when Akpon had one of his outbursts, one of the neighbours called the police. Before the police arrived, the neighbour knocked on the door and asked if I wanted to go over to his place. I took one look at the guy in his boxer shorts and decide to just stay out on the communal hallway between the flats. I was really hoping that he would go into our flat and try to calm things down. When the police arrived, Akpon had left the apartment. I was shaking as if I had done something wrong. The two police officers (one male, one female), on realising how nervous I was tried as best they could to calm me down and explained that they had come in my support.

They told me that several people die from abuse in their homes. I kept looking at the floor with my head going in circles. I was just thinking, *Okay, seriously these guys want me to turn Akpon in? When he leaves that cell or jail, I will be dead meat.* The officers asked me what I wanted to do, as they could take the baby and I into a battered women's shelter. I calmly replied that I wanted us to work things out. They left me a contact card should I change my mind later.

Soon after this event, Akpon visited a number of my relatives and explained that I had travelled, possibly out of London, with our child, and he did not quite know where I had gone. He has been trying to reach me but to no avail. Naturally, my relatives were worried and concerned for my safety and that more so of the baby as this was totally uncharacteristic of me. One of my aunts suggested he file a missing person's report, but he quickly mentioned I had been in touch with a couple of my friends, so he knew I was fine.

Only God knows what he was planning. About a week after he visited with an aunt of mine, she met me at a vegetable market. She called me out so loudly, a number of people stopped to see who it was. "Oh my goodness! Where did you go and when did you get back?" she asked as she pulled me over to a quiet spot.

"Go where?" I asked rather amused. "I have not travelled."

"Oh, really? Akpon visited us the other day and told us you left with Adiel, went out of London and had not got in touch."

"Really?" I responded very, very, very puzzled.

Before I could say another word, my aunt then said, "You are looking very poorly. You don't have to tell me you are not in a good place, it is written all over you." For the first time in over 3 years of marriage, I decided to open up to a family member.

Right there in the vegetable market on the side of the

road, I told my aunt all that I have been going through. We spent over an hour chatting. She could not believe I had been suffering in silence. In conclusion, she assured me that she will share things with my uncle, and they will come over to hear what Akpon has to say.

Broken Silence

Without announcing they were coming, my aunt and uncle turned up at the apartment on me letting them know it was a good time. Akpon was so taken aback when they arrived. He was somewhat speechless and confused. Anyway, he played along. After settling in, my uncle cleared his throat and very seriously mentioned that he has come to the realisation of the state of our marriage, and he is not happy. As soon as he started talking, Akpon took a seat that strategically positioned him in the centre of the room.

My uncle invited him to have a say and explain things from his perspective. I sat quietly in my chair, hands folded, not totally convinced of a favourable outcome of the 'peace talks' albeit hoping against hope. I look at Akpon's face, and his disposition was as if he had on a stone mask. Clearly, he wasn't in the mood of peace or harmony. His words in response still ring in my ears. His tone was cruel and cutting. He emotionlessly said that I wasn't his type, and he never should have married me. He went on to say he wasn't attracted to me and doesn't desire me. He callously explained that he is drawn to fair, voluptuous women, and in his estimation, I am as 'flat as an ironing board.' He urged my uncle to advise me to gain some weight, and we can reconvene a further discussion after that. My uncle feeling totally disrespected, hastily called the meeting to a close, thanked Akpon for his time and got up and left.

Needless-to-say after that visit, things were so frosty that we hardly spoke. One day when he came home, he suggested that I start paying him £75 a week as rent for Adiel and I. In response, I clearly told him I will not pay rent to my husband to live in our marital home. Autumn was drawing to a close, and it had started getting chilly, so we needed the heating on intermittently. Akpon banned me from putting the heating on until he decided it was cold enough to warrant heating. I would sneak around and put on the heating when he wasn't home and have extra blankets for night time if the temperatures plummeted. One morning, I needed to bathe Adiel as we had an early appointment. It was freezing! I went and put the heating on without 'permission.' Akpon got up aggressively from the room where he was sleeping and switched it off.

I went back quietly without saying a word and switched it on again. This continued a few more times, and finally, Akpon lost it. Once when I got up to put on the thermostat, he crept up behind me and slapped me right across my head. I was so unprepared for this that I fell over while using my tongue to check if all my teeth were still intact. While I was down on the ground, he kicked me and punched me a several times while saying over and over, "I have had enough of you."

It was terrible. He was so enraged. He picked up a little table on which we had some flowers in the hallway and smashed it on my foot. The table went to pieces.

At this time, our son was on the ground crying. I attempted to get up to get him and realised I could put my weight on my foot. The pain in my foot was excruciating. In a matter of minutes, my foot was twice its size. Akpon called the emergency services, requesting an ambulance. I will never forget how I had to drag myself across the floor to pick up Adiel who was only six months old and yet was crying so much I wondered if he understood what was happening.

As soon as the paramedics arrived, Akpon went out to meet them and said, "My wife fell down."

They came and took me to the hospital. After x-rays were done in the foot, it was confirmed that one of my metatarsals was broken. The doctor asked what had happened, and I went along with the story of a fall as I feared for my life at this point.

The doctor looked at me and said, "It is not medically possible for you to break your bone the way you have from a fall. You need to let us know what really happened. By the way, why have you got bruises over your face and body? I can get the police involved if you want to press charges."

I was bruised from the kicking and punching. It was evident I had not fallen, and this was my golden opportunity to press charges, yet again, I let fear hold me back. My foot was put in a cast, and I was sent home. A cousin of mine moved in with me to help with caring for the baby. At this stage, the news of my failing marriage was public knowledge in our church, within my family, and among my friends. The shame and embarrassment were weights that were too heavy to carry.

After I healed, Akpon walked in and said he had given up the apartment. This was on a Thursday. "The housing association wants their keys on Tuesday next week. You will have to find where to live. I have not been paying the rent, and they have asked for the keys, and I have cancelled the tenancy agreement."

"We have nowhere to go Akpon!" I broke down in tears. This was the ultimate betrayal. In four days, I was going to be homeless with a seven-month old baby. I started reaching out to friends to see who would put us up.

At this point I had left work to explore business opportunities that I had been working on, so I did not have a steady income. Even though I had furnished our apartment, I realised that in order for me to be accepted into someone's home, I will not need to move with all my things. I began to put together the bare essentials I needed for the foreseeable future. All my earthly belongings were in three black bags. I finally heard from one of my good friends who lived in a one-bedroom house.

The space was small, and money was tight, so we had to be patient with each other and make do with what we have. Looking back, however, this season ushered so much happiness in my life. We had so much laughter. She had a single bed, so Adiel slept on that while she and I slept on the floor. One night, the makeshift wardrobe in the room that we had constructed for my clothes collapsed on top of us as we lay on the floor. Adiel thought it was hilarious and shrieked with laughter from the comfort of the bed as we made our way out from under the heap of clothes. Fond memories of carefree times.

It didn't take long to punctuate these times as I began to receive numerous bills that Akpon had incurred on my behalf. My name was on everything as at the start of our marriage right until our separation, Akpon did not have a good credit score. So everything that required a credit check, my name went down. Unbeknownst to me, Akpon had taken liberties and run the telephone bill—calling abroad indiscriminately. There were rent, areas, etc. I found myself in £6000 debt.

Akpon found out where I had moved and came by to see us one day. We ended up having sex. The very next day, I saw him with a girlfriend of his and had flashbacks on the STD I had. I became totally paranoid that I was infected as we had used no protection. I booked an appointment with my GP. I turned up and blurted out, "I think I am HIV positive." My GP tried to convince me that she did not think I had contracted anything.

Nonetheless, she booked me into a GU clinic after a few days that tested me anonymously. I asked my friend (with whom I lived) to accompany me. We went there, and I got tested and was told to return for my results in four hours. Those were the longest four hours ever. My whole life flashed in front of me as I contemplated an early death, leaving a young child. My friend asked that we go wait at a KFC restaurant close by.

My response was, "I might be dying and all you can think about is eating chicken?" My friend could not stop laughing. Making me laugh too. I like the way she was able to lighten the mood and make me laugh so much. We returned in the time stipulated, and to my relief, I was not HIV positive. Life moved on.

Some nine months after our separation, Akpon visited, and I thought I'd bring up some of the abuse I suffered at his hands. Akpon looked at me squarely and said, "I think I suffer from amnesia because cannot recollect anything you are talking about." There was absolutely no remorse whatsoever from him. I decided at that point that I was going to file for divorce and finalise our separation. I saw a lawyer the following week and kicked off divorce proceedings. She filed the necessary papers, and this started a 2-year process of legalising our separation and divorcing myself from Akpon.

It was a long drawn, bitter, acrimonious, and nasty divorce. The pain I went through during these times was indescribable. The case was infiltrated with lies and false accusations. At a point, Akpon started insinuating I was mentally derailed, and nothing I have told the court could be relied on. His legal representation had to advise him that mental instability against a spouse was not a door one would want to open in a divorce proceeding. There were times when the pain in my heart was so intense that I was surprised to wake up some mornings.

The sense of rejection and abandonment, the feelings of failure, the dark cloud of disappointment, the shame and disgrace seemed to envelop my every thought, breeding feelings of insecurity and low self-worth. There were days when I could not get out of bed, and for days, I would not go to work. I refused to look at myself in the mirror for days. At this point, I convinced myself life was not worth living and became extremely suicidal. I called my brother Joe and had what he recalls as a very strange conversation. I asked about pain free ways to die. I thought through slashing my wrist. I thought about taking my car to an enclosed place and inhaling the fumes from the engine.

I once went to London Bridge and contemplated jumping as I watched the flow of the Thames. Every time I thought about no longer living, I thought about my little Adiel and decided to live—for him. He became my lifeline, the reason

I would get out of bed. But that did not shift the depression. I began to think that if there was a way to end it all for Adiel, then voila, problem solved. So one day, I went to the chemist and bought a whole lot of over the counter sleeping tablets. I decided that would lace my son's milk and get him to sleep off. When I realise he no longer has a pulse, I will drink mine.

My friend with whom I lived usually took him to a park on Saturdays, so before going to bed on a certain Friday night, I said to her, "Please leave the baby in the morning. We are sleeping downstairs. I just want to spend time with him tomorrow."

My head was going in circles, and I had knots in my stomach as I fell asleep. At about 5:40am, I heard my phone ringing continuously. I looked at it annoyingly before picking it up. It was my pastor!

"Hey Avril, are you sleeping?" he asked gingerly.

"Pastor, is everything okay? I am up now. The call woke me up. It is okay."

He explained he had been up since 3 am and had been praying for me. He said the devil desires to cut my life short, but God has placed an embargo on him. He declared that the light of God within me is eternal, and I must never forget that nothing, absolutely nothing, can separate me from the love of God. Neither death nor life, neither angels nor demons, neither height nor depth, neither things present nor things to come.

He spoke to me for an hour and all God used him to do was to remind me of His unfailing love for me. I fell to me knees and wept like a baby. "I was going to end it all today, Pastor. The pain and the disappointment are unquantifiable. I cannot feel God's love. I feel like I am in a very dark pit and can't find a way out." I spoke when I could catch my breath in my crying.

The pastor prayed with me and rebuked the vain thoughts and imaginations. He squashed the lies and spoke life and light to my dark situation. He released me to live and to declare the works of God. What a powerful encounter that was. I laid on the floor a good while after the conversation.

My friend and host came downstairs and met me on the floor. It was obvious I had been crying. As she had done on many occasions, she knelt down beside me and gave me a big hug without saying a word. I held on to her and sobbed. I looked at her and said, "I KNOW God loves me. He loves me so very, very much!"

"That's right." she said. "I know that too. Avril, everything is going to be okay."

"Please take the baby out. I have changed my mind and now want to spend time with God. I just want to be in His presence."

We had breakfast, did our Saturday morning clean up, got Adiel ready, and as they had done every Saturday, left for the park. When they left, it was 1:00pm. I went to my CD collection and took a Fred Hammond album titled *Pages of Life Chapters I & II*. I laid on the carpet in the living room and just allowed myself to drift into the presence of God. When the album got to the 6th song—"Please do not pass me by," I began to weep. I reached the CD player and hit the repeat button. I began to talk to God just like I did at the age of 10 on the back steps of my house. "God, where are you?" I spoke to God as a friend, as a father, as the lover of my soul, as the preserver of my sanity, as the ray of hope that was penetrating my present darkness, as the anchor for me that has kept me in the storms of life. I just let that song speak to a deep place within me.

I began to realise that Jesus loved me in a way that was revelatory and revolutionary even when I could not love myself. His light flooded my soul. I prayed from my belly, and suddenly, I began to feel a bubbling from within me. I felt a stirring. Something supernatural was happening to me. I began to flow with the spirit of God in such alignment—it was like two birds in a love dance. I felt something eject from within me, and suddenly, I felt joy, deep inexplicable joy. I had nothing to be happy about, yet I had so much joy.

Finally, I looked up, and it was 6pm! I had been on the floor for 6 hours. Not a single call came in on my phone. I had not felt the need for the loo. There was absolutely no distraction. I simply had encountered God! How things had shifted in the way they did could only be the work of God. When I looked around, the house seemed brand new. I got up, walked the mirror, and realised how dishevelled my hair was and how much weight I had lost. I took a good look at myself and realised my legs were now bow-legged. Instead of throwing a pity party at my miserable state, I spoke the following words out aloud, "Avril, you are beautiful and a blessing to your generation." Then, as if I answered myself, I said, "I shall not die but live and declare the works of God." I left and decided to take a shower.

There was such a skip in my step and joy in my heart. I knew without a shadow of a doubt that I had hit my lowest point, and it was onwards and upwards now. My flatmate returned with Adiel. She had decided to take him to visit another friend. Had she decided to have come back after the park, I certainly would have been interrupted. I am forever grateful and humbled that God met me in a place of need. There is no pit so deep that God is not deep that God is not deeper still. There is no cloud so dark and no place so arid that God cannot reach us. My worship brought me into the presence of God and as the Bible says in Psalm 16:11: *In His presence there is fullness of Joy*. That is exactly what I had a FULLNESS of joy . . . It flushed out depression and misery.

New Beginnings

The next week, I told my friend I was ready to move out. She was very apprehensive because she had seen at first hand the depth of my pain and knew how low I had descended. She asked over and over if I felt ready to move out. I certainly was and not only that, I knew I was going to be okay. I went to the local estates agent and enquired to rent a room. I wasn't looking my best I guess, because the first thing the agent asked me was if I was alright. He went on to ask me why I was just wanting to rent a room, not a whole apartment, and if I wouldn't consider buying. I was so shocked that he wasn't asking me to rent a bigger place, but he was suggesting that I buy.

I sat this guy down as if I was in therapy and explained my current circumstance and advised him that really the best thing was for me to simply rent. He asked about my finances, and I held nothing back. He eventually said to me that I should not be in a hurry. The financial adviser went to another branch and would next be with them in a couple of days, so he asked me to come back and see him.

I left the Estates Agent quite disturbed that I may not have been clear about my situation. What could a financial adviser possibly have to say? I am broke, tired, and in debt. Anyway, I patiently waited a couple of days and turned up again at the estates agent, this time with my young son as if to drive home the point that (a) we are desperate to move the requirement for accommodation forward and (b) I am a single parent so please don't start a whole load of hairy fairy financial discussions going nowhere.

The financial adviser had a very big and welcoming smile as I entered the office. He was so warm, I instantly felt at home. He went through my finances—my income and expenditure and my impulsive spending. At that time, I had discovered retail therapy, and it temporarily fixed a few ills for me. I then had 3 or 4 store cards, and I would go clothes and shoes shopping, racking up hundreds of pounds on my card. The sense of empowerment I felt was indescribable. I would take the things home, have a good look at them, realising that I (a) couldn't afford them, (b) had no space for them, and (c) didn't really need them. I would take them back and get a refund. There were times, however, when I will not return the things and my debt grew.

He asked to see my cards and stealthily took out a large pair of scissors and cut up my cards, violating my human right in front of my eyes.

I shrieked, "Do you know what you are doing? You jerk! Who or what gives you the right to destroy my cards? What on Earth are you smoking?"

He smiled and gently reminded me I had agreed for him to help me at the start of our conversation, and he helped me understand that I needed to take charge of my finances if I ever have a fighting chance of making it in life.

As hurt as I was about the loss of my pacifier, I knew he

was speaking the truth. He said, "Look at your son. He needs a mum who will make wise decisions for him. If someone takes your stove, don't ever let them take your fire. You are a beautiful, articulate, resourceful young woman who has her whole future ahead of her. Yes, your husband was a jerk and messed up but don't take the baton from him and self-destruct."

I looked up at him, and through my tears, I thanked him sincerely. I knew that if I had the courage to live, God will give me the best life I could have. I started putting my things together when I realised that actually, the adviser did not tell me about the room I wanted to rent. Before I could speak, he interrupted my thoughts and asked whether my friend will put me up for a further six months. He promised me that if I let him help me, not only will I be able to clear my debts, but he will see that I purchase my first home.

This man was so kind, so affirmative, and gave me so much hope, I decided to take this six-month challenge. I went back home and shared my experience with my friend and host, and she gladly extended her roof to me for a further 6 month. She was happy to have our continued companionship, and I will never be able to pay her for her kindness to me and my then infant son at what was the neediest times of my life.

Six months came and went very quickly. I had to submit myself to this financial adviser, disclosing every financial decision and action I took. I cultivated a lot of financial discipline in this season of my life. I had to see this man regularly who was a perfect stranger but to whom I had become very accountable. In a sense, it felt so good to have someone dependable who kept their word and did not have a hidden agenda. Sometimes, I had to pinch myself that he was human not an angel. To this day well after this guy has retired, he remains a personal friend.

Within a year, my debts were cleared. Although I still had a bad credit, I managed to get a mortgage agreement in principle and decide to grab the opportunity to buy my first home. This, in itself, was miraculous to me. I started looking for a place to buy. There was such a boost of confidence in my heart. As I looked, I found this lovely cottage that was just perfect for us. I learnt that I was competing with an established builder who was looking to buy a handful of houses in the road for a development. It had to take a miracle as they had approached the sellers and offered more money than the house was on the market for.

The couple favoured Adiel and I and was compassionately disposed toward us. In spite of the offer of more money, the couple selling insisted on selling their house to us. I did not sleep all night when the sale completed. God, yet again, had demonstrated his love, fatherhood, and covering to me unequivocally.

Hope Renewed

Our moving date was set, and we moved. I had acquired a little bit more than the 3 black bags that represented all my worldly possessions at the time of my separation from Akpon.

We moved and were met with the kindest neighbours. God was yet again surrounding us with favour. The neighbour on our left quickly cooked us a meal when they realised we were moving in and brought us some hot lunch. The neighbour on the right came over, introduced himself, and offered to mow our lawn. I was floored by the kindness from these perfect strangers I experienced. In our first conversation, I learnt the lady on our left had young kids at the nursery I had enrolled Adiel in, so she kindly offered to drop him off and pick him up as and when she takes her kids. There was, therefore, no need to rush from work (which was a 2-hour drive away) or panic if I got stuck in traffic.

Janet reached for the lemonade and realised as they had been so mesmerised by Avril's story, they had drank the lot of it. "Gosh, how long have we been here? Let me put a quick call out to hubby and let him know I will not be back anytime soon" she said.

"Well, that went down a storm" Avril remarked. "Let me get a refill."

Rosa got up for a bathroom break, stretched her legs, noting what an amazing journey Avril had been on. Janet and Rosa conversed as Avril made some more lemonade, and they resettled back for the continuation.

"I can't wait to find out how you got to where you are now. God is good uh? Who would have thought you have been through such hell and high water?"

"Sit tight and hang in there guys. It gets more interesting. I am so thankful that God does not define us by our present circumstances but that he looks beyond faults, sees our needs, and deals with us according to the destinies he prepared for us" Avril responded.

When we moved in, we had very little, and Adiel and I slept on the living room floor. In spite of our circumstances, I could see that God was putting my life back together one chapter at a time. My tears slowly became laughter. Adiel had the kids in the neighbourhood to play with, and he was so very happy. I began to accumulate material things, and life was taking shape.

I began to miss adult company and longed for my mother's companionship, and frankly, with the completion of my masters degree on the horizon, I needed her help too. My friend who had hosted us continued to be of great help and would step in, in a heartbeat whenever I needed her.

One day, I woke up to the disturbing news that a civil war had hit Freetown. The atrocities to human life were so great, one couldn't effectively articulate. Rebel forces entered the city and violated humanity in what was dubbed the bloodiest civil war in history. Pregnant women had babies cut out of their stomachs prematurely, people were maimed by having their hands or arms and feet or legs cut off. Kids were orphaned by having their parents killed in front of them and then drugged and recruited as child soldiers. A good percentage of the population fled to neighbouring countries as refugees. People were killed senselessly and indiscriminately, and for a good few weeks, I could not locate my mother. Finally, she got in touch and was in Gambia. I flew down with Adiel to go see her and made arrangements with her for her to join us in the UK.

A month after, we returned from Gambia. Mum arrived in the UK. We spent endless nights in conversations as she replayed the horror of the war. I had a lot to tell her two of my personal hell, and she was so hurt that I had gone through so much. In the first week that she arrived, I remember her looking into my wardrobe and asking, "Where are your clothes?" and walking into the kitchen realising I actually owned very little. Not to mention that we did not have sofas or any chairs in the living room. We and our guests actually sat on the floor.

"I got this, Mum" I assured her in a conversation. "My financial adviser friend, has taught me how to prioritise my spending and how to cut my coat according to my size. I buy stuff as I can afford it. I have this six-month plan to start procuring the things we need to make this house a home."

"Well, at least let me handle shopping and the food budget" Mum suggested. "I have learnt in life how to make a little go a long way."

So mum took administrative responsibility of grocery shopping, and I took care of everything else as we began to form the framework of a new family unit. Adiel was bowled over to have his grand mum around who spoilt him rotten.

Things stabilised as we got some normalcy and routine to life. Out of the blue, we were hit by another calamity. There were rumblings at work about the company not hitting the expected targets and that could only mean a reshuffling of roles, dissolving of departments and teams, and loss of jobs.

I remember the meeting we had at work and how I shivered as I thought of the responsibility I shouldered. The whole meeting left me sick in my stomach. I just wanted to know without all the waffle what was going to happen to us. Finally, they announced that our team was facing the chop, and we were going to be paid for 3 months as a garden leave in which we were free to search for other opportunities. I was unemployed and totally unprepared for this blow. I was so shocked at how my life could change in such a jiffy that I couldn't even cry.

While I was in this dilemma, one day out of the blue, I had a letter from the courts that Akpon had filed charges against me for withholding our child from him. I could not believe my eyes. We had not seen him for years, where was this coming from?

I turned up at court super early, hoping to grab a moment with him. I saw him, and he had a devilish smile. I walked up to him and ask that we step out for a moment. "What are you playing at?" I asked angrily.

"Well I have a right to see my son, don't I? And frankly I feel you have been all over the place as if the boy doesn't have a father."

I took a deep breath, trying to process what was happening. "Surely you know where we live because you got the court to send me the papers there. Why did you not come round to see him if you are that desperate? Why a court proceeding Akpon? Haven't you troubled me enough? You have never been interested in Adiel. Fair enough if you want to be a part of his life, I wouldn't stop you but why drag me through a legal mud path?"

He had a smirk on his face as he responded, "See that's why I like you 'legal mud path.' I like that expression because that is what it is. Get ready for battle."

We walked back in, and our case was called. The judge read the preliminary statement and asked my side of the claim. I explained that I had neither seen Akpon nor heard from him so why I was in court was baffling to me. I asked for mediation to see if we could agree something without a full blown long drawn battle. A mediation meeting was arranged, and everything I suggested, Akpon refused.

Within days of leaving that meeting, I had several calls from people we mutually knew asking me why I would want Akpon back. I was amazed. I explained that I had been summoned to court on the allegation of stopping him from seeing our son. Akpon had taken pains to explain to mutual friends of ours that me suggesting he visits Adiel in our home, was my ploy to get Adiel used to him in a move on him to get back with him.

As we could not reach an agreement in mediation, the matter was referred back to the court. The judge ruled that he should have a 30-minute visitation every other Saturday for six months to start off with. It became six hellish months as again and again and again Akpon disappointed Adiel with a no show several times over.

This season stressed me out so very much. Once as I was in a conversation with a relative of mine in America, he suggested I hop over for a break. It had just been such a roller coaster, one thing after another. Coupled with that a dear friend of mine of many years was getting married and had chosen Adiel for a page boy.

We stacked up and left travelling to Atlanta for the wedding and travelled thereafter by road to Minnesota where we settled. On leaving, I told Akpon I was going to explore work opportunities in the U.S. He was at liberty to see his child whenever he chose to. All he needed was to give me some notice, and I will facilitate a meet up. He joyfully agreed. At this point, it had come to light that his sudden interest in being in contact with Adiel was because he was about to remarry and wanted to paint the picture of a responsible father to his future wife. Even at this point, he had never paid child support.

We settled in reasonably well into the U.S., and it was a breath of fresh air from all the recent drama in my life. I got Adiel enrolled in a private school, and he was happy, but he missed the UK so very much. In the mind of a then 5-year old, he couldn't just process where his friends had gone and why we were in a different country. In a matter of months, his accent had changed, and he sounded very American.

All my paternal family live in the U.S. My father's siblings live within driving distance of each other in the same state, so it was a joy to bond with that side of the family and to explore the American culture first hand. I would often have to go up into Canada to process my immigration extensions as I could only legally stay in the US for 90 days at a time until my status would have changed to something more permanent.

Akpon and I kept in touch via email. He wrote now and again, and in those sporadic conversations, I updated him as much as I could about Adiel's development.

One day, I got a strange email from a lawyer saying that he had been contacted by Akpon, and Akpon was worried as he did not know the whereabouts of his son. Again, It was very deeply troubling to put it mildly especially that we had been in dialogue via email a few days prior. I responded to the lawyer that maybe he had the wrong person, seeing we had been in touch, and Akpon knew where we were. I had no further communications from him. I forwarded the mail to Akpon enquiring if indeed he had seen a lawyer and heard nothing back.

The following weekend I was due to make a trip to Winnipeg in Canada to get our visas extended. One of my cousins opted to drive me, and we packed for the weekend and left. The drive up the great lake was beautiful, scenic, and breath-taking, and I was privileged to experience it in all seasons. This was the thick of winter, and it was postcard beautiful. My cousin Aaron and I enjoyed some lovely tunes, and it was such a memorable trip as we spoke lots. It's amazing how very little quality time one gets when life gets busy.

After 4 hours on the road, we got to the Canadian/US border. As usual, we were asked for our passports. Very unusually however, we were asked to step outside the vehicle, and I felt some commotion as the officers surrounded the car and called for backup. I heard them saying, "we have located her, we have located her." As soon as I stepped outside the vehicle, an armed officer read me my rights and ushered me to a waiting area in the booth.

My head was going in circles. "Ma'am you are under arrest, anything you say or do can be used against you in a court of law."

I felt as if my vision was blurred for a minute. I calmly asked through the tears that clouded my eyes, "What am I arrested for please?"

"International child kidnapping." Little did I know that there was an international warrant issued for my arrest as my ex-husband had made a claim in the international court of law that I had taken our child out of the jurisdiction of the UK without his knowledge and permission.

I couldn't believe my ears. How can someone kidnap their own child? Surely this can't be legal. I was processed as a charged criminal and thrown into a cell. I was so devastated by the experience I went totally hysterical, especially when I overheard that plans were being made to separate Adiel and I so that he can stay with a foster family until a hearing is set and I see a judge. I completely lost my cool. At one point, one of the officers asked me to sit down. I told him I had been sat in a car for 4 hours, and now, I am falsely accused of kidnapping my own child. The last thing on my mind is sitting down!

He cocked his gun and said quite affirmatively, "Ma'am I am asking you again to please sit down. If you do not co-operate with a police officer, I might have to break your legs."

My cousin went on his knees and started to plead with me to sit. So I sat down. All my personal effects were taken from me. I was handcuffed and treated like a criminal.

My cousin calmly went up to the desk and asked if the UK high commission could be called. I was put on the phone to the consul—a lady and explained what had happened. She asked me to stay calm and say nothing and that legal help will be on the way. In two hours, a lawyer arrived. He took my statement and opened negotiations at a national level.

At one point, he requested I be passed on to the Canadian government as apparently due to some commonwealth agreement, I would have had a much easier time with the law. That request was turned down, stating that I had allegedly committed a crime on U.S. soil. Eventually, a deal was struck that I would be extradited back to the UK to face my charges, and if found guilty, I would pay a fine of £250,000 and be sent back to face up to 20 years in an American jail. The next day, a number of my family members drove up to the border to investigate my plight. They were disallowed from seeing me. While awaiting extradition, and realising that my family wanted answers, I was moved to a house in North Dakota where I spent several days in house arrest with the company of about 8 police officers. When I once enquired how long I was going to be kept there, the answer was cold and brutal.

"Till an airline agrees to fly you back for free." I had no access to the internet or to my bank accounts. I was only allowed a couple of calls a day. So I called one of my uncles and asked him to get a cousin of mine to buy us tickets. Our tickets were bought, flights arranged, and I was scheduled to fly home in a matter of days. In those dark days, I learnt a true dimension of what it means to be comforted by the Holy Spirit. I was literally woken up on occasion and directed to passages of scripture. It was amazing. Most of the day while I was alone, I'd get on my knees and spend time in worship especially that I had experience closeness with God in worship in my previous encounter. There was such a powerful and real closeness that I felt with God in that season.

We were escorted to the airport in Minnesota while I was handcuffed to an officer. I had lived for a few weeks in same clothes and underwear I had packed only for a weekend trip. My things were as they had been left—untouched and unpacked. I called Adiel's school and whipped up a lie that there was a family emergency that needed to be taken care of, so I needed to travel urgently and will be relocating him back to the UK. As long as I live, I will find it hard to forget the humiliation I felt when we went to the airport, and I was treated like a criminal.

I was the last passenger to get on the plane, and it was only when I got boarded that the handcuffs were taken off. I still had not seen my passport from when it was taken from me during the arrest at the border. I kept thinking *what if I turn up in the UK and they do not have my passport?* Anyway, it was a red eye flight, and I slept most of it. When the plane landed, I was so happy to be back on home soil.

We were escorted off the flight and handed over to ground staff. The whole thing felt so very strange. Thankfully, a nice and welcoming immigration officer met me at the airport. "So what happened with you, young lady across the pond?" he asked jokingly.

I went into a long-winded explanation of what happened.

To my surprise, he cut me short, pulled out our passports and said, "The Queen welcomes you home. Don't mind those Yankees." I was so appreciative of his humour and kindness to me I gave him a big warm hug.

I walked out and met my mum. She was so emotional. On seeing his grandma, Adiel broke loose from my hold and ran straight into her arms. We stood at the airport for a good few minutes in a group hug. It was so powerful. The love and acceptance that I felt from my mother at that moment was indescribable. She kept whispering over and over again, "I am so happy you are home. Everything is going to be OK. I am so sorry for what you have been through." In the days to come, it became evident to me that my barometer of security was seriously damaged. I was deeply, deeply traumatised. To this day, I hate enclosed spaces.

In the week that followed, I appeared in court, formerly charged with International Child Kidnapping. When I turned up in court, I met Akpon with a very evil smirk on his face. As our eyes met, he grinned menacingly and whispered, "Oh you thought you can run away from me, uh?"

I walked away without a word. I sat quietly as I waited for our case to be called.

Finally, we were called, and I went back to stand in front of the judge that had reserved the matter to himself. It was nauseatingly nostalgic. I hate court rooms. The judge proceeded with our matter and enquired the validation of the case that was brought against me, giving me an opportunity to make my case. I did not have time to hire a lawyer; however, I produced the emails that had gone back and forth between Akpon and I. The case did not take 15 minutes.

The judge turned to Akpon and said, "Why did you file a case against your ex-wife citing an abduction, kidnapping of your son, and absconding to an unknown international location. I have just read your case details, Mr Akpon. Here are numerous mails to the contrary. You got this woman arrested and extradited. May I suggest to you that you are nothing but a vicious and vindictive bastard?"

Then he turned to me and said, "Where did you meet him?"

"At a bus stop, My Lord" I responded.

"Well, well, well, that says a lot. I feel sorry for you. This case has no basis. I discharge the matter. See the court clerk and do what you need to do to file the matter as null and void with the American government."

"My Lord," Akpon said respectfully, "I would like to file a case for custody."

"Then go ahead and do so. You have just wasted taxpayer's money today" the judge said, sounding quite disgusted and agitated.

In the days that followed, I went to the American Embassy and cleared my name. I was given a 10-year visa that will enable me to live or work in the U.S. in compensation.

Akpon did file a case for custody. He wasted the courts time and my time and used every trick in the book to lengthen the case. Once, he accused me of being selfish and career-minded, and his suggestion was for the courts to make an order to take our son into the care system.

On another occasion, knowing my mum was helping me with Adiel, he came up with an allegation that my mother was a paedophile and a child abuser, but unfortunately, the records were destroyed in the civil war in Sierra Leone. Again, these allegations were dismissed as baseless. It took another 4 years for the case to be completed. In this time, he sought contact and physically abused our son.

After numerous court hearings, involvement with Social Services and psychological assessments that Adiel had to go through, at what turned out to be the final hearing, the judge asked Akpon, "Are you satisfied that you have presented all your arguments to this court?"

"I haven't made up my mind yet that I want the case to be completed" was Akpon's response.

The judge was clearly irritated. He looked at Akpon and said sternly, "If after 4 years you haven't made up your mind, then the court will make it up for you." The judge looked at the lawyers and wrapped up the matter in a few sentences. After 6 years of humiliation, tears, and mockery of the court system, I got full custody of our son. Finally, I was able to close Akpon's chapter and move on.

In the meantime, my career blossomed. But what this season of my life taught me also while I was seeing the true ugliness and depravity of the man I had loved enough to commit my life to, I had been dating, and I was fast learning what I certainly DO NOT want in a man.

NOT—"THE ONE"

Most people have a checklist of what they desire in a mate. I did too. I have had so many encounters, some of which had nothing to do with a checklist.

In the year mum re-joined me in the UK, I decided to surprise her for her birthday by flying the family to the Bahamas. It was beautiful because up until the day we were leaving, Mum had no clue where we were going. Adiel was too young to care less—he just went with the flow, but Mum's excitement was uncontainable.

Up until that point, I had had very interesting emotional experiences, and I had put myself in some ridiculous situations.

As a young girl, I had always been very chaste and only desired to share the very deep areas of my heart and experience the fulfilment of my sexual fantasies with only one man. I had resolved to give the best of myself to my husband. So it was a real shame that my marriage ended the way it did. Still in my twenties, with raging emotions and a strong desire to love and to be loved in return, I found myself in all sorts of relationships that I am sure you guys might or might not be able to identify with.

Rosa, being such a tease chuckled and said, "Please tell us

girl. I am sure this bit is really going to give us the tickles." She leaned back with a big grin on her face.

Shock and Awe

Now as a woman who was single and ready to mingle, I was shocked and in awe that some of the most perverted demographic of men are those behind the pulpit. People who are called to shepherd a flock, people of God. When I became a Christian, I was a very young girl. Very impressionable. I looked up to my pastors for spiritual guidance and direction. Naively, I felt that spiritual leaders were exempt from certain distractions in life. The first church I found myself in was a small church with membership fluctuating from 30—50 parishioners, mostly West Africans.

The pastor started visiting me rather regularly and at really odd times. There was an occasion when he came and picked me up and told me to go out with him, that there was something he wanted to show me. We drove for about an hour and then veered off into some dark country lanes. At every juncture when I asked where we were going, he simply responded, "Somewhere special. I want to show you something. You are going to love it."

After a further fifteen minutes driving through fields, a police car that had been following us flashed us down.

The police ran a security check on his car and asked if I was okay. He then asked what we were doing in such a remote part of town at that time of night. The pastor just mumbled that we were going for a drive. The police remarked what a strange place to be taking a drive as there were no streetlights. I am sure that was divine intervention as he decided to turn around after the encounter with the police. On other occasions, he turned up at 1:00am, claiming he was on his way home from some appointment and was checking on people to see if they are okay, so he just wanted to make a pit stop at mine. I actually thought to myself that this was totally unethical.

I just did not expect that the pastor of the church with a beautiful wife and two kids would be seeking an extra marital affair within such a small church community. So the last conclusion I drew on these frequent trips was that this guy was seeking an affair. I expressed that I was uncomfortable with his late night visits and that I don't thrive with broken sleep. He made his visit less frequent and earlier. Often time, there was no objective.

One night, he turned up at my house close to midnight. I was already for bed and thought something must have happened. So as soon as he turned up, I asked if he was okay. Then, he said he just thought about me and decided to bring me some strawberry cheesecake.

"At this time? Couldn't that wait until tomorrow?"

Before I could complete my sentence, the pastor grabbed me and started to kiss my neck. I was horrified.

The next day I called a friend who also happened to be a member of the Board of the church. I thought I had to tell someone. I battled with whether I would be believed. Anyway, I trusted Mark enough and opened up to him. As I spoke, he hung his head and shook it in dismay momentarily. "I will speak to him in private and if I have no success, I will take another Board member to address the matter. Should we still not have a way forward, I will take the matter to the Board. This has so stop. This is not the first time." He assured me he will do his best to ensure things are dealt with. I felt a weight lift off my shoulders. I was so relieved that at least I was believed.

I was kept posted with developments, and the matter went all the way to the board. When the matter was addressed at Board level, the best the pastor could come up with was that in his estimation, I was possessed with a seductive demon. His frequent visits were to ascertain that and to deliver me if there was a manifestation.

I left the church immediately.

I went to another mega church with three thousand members. My thinking was that surely this new church will be so much more established that there will be none of this sexual perversion. How wrong was I? The assistant pastor took a liking to me and over time, began to visit me at home. I thought nothing of it because at this time, I lived with my mum, and we would all sit and chat. He was married with five children. He brought his wife over often time, and over time, it felt like our families were blending. Coming from different cultures, our meetings were always centred on food. We traded recipes, and I felt quite comfortable with him. One of his sons coincidentally had the same name as my son.

We would often need to have meetings as he was directly responsible for the department within which I served. Secularly, he has administration of a few retirement homes near where I lived. When he realised that, he would often drop by our home, say a quick hello and leave. One day however, when he came, he decided to stay a lot longer than he normally did. We were sitting in the kitchen, and then, he reached out and held my hands and looked seductively in my eyes. He then said, "If I wasn't married, I would propose to you. In fact, if God permitted polygamy, I would make you my second wife." I began to be suspicious of his motives.

One day, I had a call from him that there was something rather urgent he wanted to discuss with me. I drove all the way to Essex where he lived, over an hour's drive from mine. When I arrived, I was surprised that he was home alone because usually the kids are outside playing on a summer's day. It was ghostly quiet. I parked my car and walked across to the house. As I approached the house, he leaned against the door post and looked at me seductively.

Then he said, "Oh my God. You look so very sexy. I can just imagine what you would look like in bathing suit."

I was not sure my ears heard right. So I asked him to repeat what he said.

In response, he said, "if only God would allow polygamy, I would marry you in a heartbeat." He then pinned me up against the wall and tried to kiss me. It then dawned on me that this was a setup, and he had waited for an opportunity when his family was not around to make a pass at me. Thank God I had not gone into the house.

I slapped this man so hard my hand hurt. I made a quick dash for my car and sped off. I stayed home from church for over a month, devastated, and confused that married men in such a place of authority could be so perverted. My perspective was changing, and my brain could not process that integrity is such a rare attribute.

In that same church, I was great friends with one of the youth leaders. He would often travel back and forth to Nigeria for business, and we had great rapport. Once when he was coming over to the UK to spend time with his family, he called and asked if we would hang out one evening. I consented, and he turned up on the day we had agreed.

We took a short drive to a restaurant, and to my surprise, when we settled, my friend ordered a bottle of red wine. He had made me believe he did not drink alcohol. He drank the whole bottle over the evening. I constantly asked him if he was fit to drive, and he did not feel in any way compromised. Thankfully, he safely got me back home and asked if he could come in to have a quick strong coffee before heading back as it was quite late, and he thought he had overeaten a bit. I graciously allowed him and walked toward the kitchen to pop the kettle. Suddenly, he grabbed me, pinned me up against the wall, frantically tried to kiss me while putting his hand down my blouse as he reached for my breast. I fought and shouted over and over, "No, No, No."

In the process, he ripped my buttons on my blouse, and after scratching his face, he relented and simply walked out to his car and drove off.

I closed the door and fell to the floor and cried my eyes out. In the morning, I called a friend of mine who worked for the police and asked if I could press charges. He explained that as we had gone out together, and I had let him back in and he did not rape me, it might be tricky to file a case of sexual harassment, which is what I felt—harassed, betrayed by a friend and violated.

In the days that followed, I replayed our friendship and the good times we had had and wondered how it could all go so horribly wrong. He tried to call me several times, but

I gave him no audience. Finally, after a week, I got a mail from him that read:

My dear Avril,
*   I knew what transpired last Friday had triggered issues once I noticed you had stopped picking my calls. I had hoped we can talk things over the phone, but . . . .*

I am aware of the regard you accord me and our friendship, to this I do feel I have not only let you down, but also myself. My actions were inexcusable no matter what my situations are and it doesn›t matter if I am in a vulnerable place in my life or not.

I understand if you can't relate right now, I am ready to give you all the space you require, though, I would have wanted to speak with you. Please know that it's not like I allow my passion drive me to the point where I make a pass on anyone I have feelings for.

I would take whatever comes to me from you where this is concerned, but please do not judge me. As hard as this is to believe, this was the devil at work in me.

I am deeply hurt to know that you feel I have taken advantage of you in so many ways, but I lay humbly at the altar of mercy and the throne of grace, also appealing to your bowel of mercy and goodness. Please forgive me. I am still your brother and still have a lot of regard and respect for you. I confess, I should have dealt with the attraction once I noticed it. Thanks for loving me past my faults.

And just like that, years of friendship were flushed down the toilet, and this friend became a memory. In these experiences, I learnt that gifting and character are two different things and I had to 'test every spirit'. It is important to not just trust anyone just because they label themselves as men of God but to know they are living out that calling with integrity.

Philanthropy

My desire for more children grew as Adiel grew older. I often spoke with him about possibly adopting a sibling for him. So I made it a prayer point and knew that somehow God will work out an addition to our family as He sees fit. The nature of my work would not have permitted the legal adoption for a sibling for Adiel. I toyed with the idea of fostering; however, I did not want to have children only for a few months or years and after a season of bonding, have them leave us.

My mind shifted and I purposed to sponsor less fortunate children, and when we have time, we will visit when the opportunity arises. I started on the lookout for organisations that had initiatives that helped underprivileged children of African descent in various ways. I wanted an organisation that was charitable and accountable. My search lasted for over a year.

One day, I had a dream that I went to a banquet that was held in my honour and afterward, I was given a set of twins—girls. I woke up and wondered if I will one day give birth to twins. A few months after, I went to a friend mum's funeral and met another lady I had not seen in ages. I asked her how she was doing, and she said she had pretty much relocated to Sierra Leone where he had set up an orphanage for bereaved children of war victims.

She then went on to let me know they had just received

a set of twin girls and were desperate for sponsorship for them. A warm, fuzzy feeling came over me. I grabbed her and exclaimed, "You are not going to believe what I am going to say." She smiled and looked at me rather curiously, with a silence that created the space and opportunity for me to speak. I explained to her that meeting her was no coincidence. I explained my dream and the yearning I had had to impact the life of a disadvantageous child. I had such joy from being able to make a difference in this way.

A few years later, a family of four children were bereaved when Ebola broke out in Sierra Leone. I was made aware of their arrival and decided to sponsor them as well. So from desiring to help one child, here I was helping 6 in the space of a few years. Once I called a friend in Sierra Leone, and as we spoke, she was visited by an old Ghanaian friend of hers whom she had met a few years back. He told the guy that she was on the phone with me, and I was in the UK, so if he doesn't mind, she will want to finish her conversation.

On realising my friend was running the risk of being socially awkward I decided its best we end the conversation. The friend of hers then said, "Why don't I say hello?" This very funny guy came on the phone and made me laugh so much. It was like we had known each other a long time. Just before we said our goodbyes, he said he felt that I should contact a friend of his in the U.S. He didn't know why but felt it was good for us to be connected. I called his friend Joe in a matter of days who had also been told he should expect a call from me. It was a very awkward conversation as neither of us knew why we were being asked to contact each other. After exchanging pleasantries, he blurted out, "I am a married man with 6 children."

I chuckled in response and said, "I have a son." We spoke about work and family, and then the conversation drifted to my love and passion of helping orphans. He then breathed deeply and told me he had an orphanage that he was about to close because frankly, he was fed up as his nuclear family had grown.

I decided to fly to Ghana to check out the orphanage. He connected me a friend of his who arranged to meet me at the airport and helped with all the logistics to ensure my stay was smooth. I landed in Accra, and it was warm and beautiful. I had a very warm welcome and a very pleasant stay. I enjoyed the food and the kindness of the people. I felt I could live in Accra in a heartbeat. The city was loud and colourful, yet the sense of peace and security was unequalled in my many travels. I visited the orphanage. The angelic kids had prepared me welcome banners and sang songs as I got out of the car. I burst into tears with gratitude in my heart. It was a no brainer that I was connected to these kids, and I was going to do whatever it took to help them.

When I was there, I decided to visit a church next to the hotel on the Sunday. I walked into the deafening but vibrant music and stood in awe of how expressive people were as they worshipped. It was a sight to behold. The dancing was contagious and although most of the songs were sung in the local dialect (Twi) which I did not understand, however, my soul appreciated the connection it created to God. As the worship service proceeded, people left their seats and danced waving white handkerchiefs in the air. That is culturally how Ghanaians hail and honour their chiefs and kings.

As was customary, all first timers were asked to stand so that they were given a special welcome. The pastor announced that he would like to meet us all (about 4 of us) in the back after the service. I thought it was very kind of him. He met us after the service, and to my surprise, he asked me to wait so he can have a personal word. I stayed behind in good faith. The pastor then met me when the church was almost over, and there were barely any members in the premises. He then asked if I was from the U.S. or the UK and where I stayed. I was quite perturbed by his personal interest especially when he said he will pop over to the hotel in a couple of days to pay me a visit.

I wondered whether this was the VIP treatment that all first timers receive. In a couple of days, true to his word, he visited at 7pm and asked for me at the reception. I had a call in my room that I had a guest. Initially, I couldn't connect the name, so I got dressed and headed downstairs. He then said if I wouldn't mind he will take me round for a drive as I was a foreigner. Innocently, I went on this drive with him. He drove me right out of the city to a place he called his hideout. I used the time to talk to him about the church, his ministry, how he got things started etc. Having spent all my life in church, there was a lot to talk about. When we got to our destination, it was obvious this was somewhere he was well known at. He ordered drinks, and we sat down.

He seriously started hitting on me. I was embarrassed for him, bewildered, and slightly confused. He kept saying he had a wife from whom he was estranged; however, he believed God was bringing us together. I told him that I was single but disinterested. He increased his persuasion, and I felt quite irritated at his lack of tact. I, however, remembered

I was in a foreign land in the middle of nowhere with a perfect stranger. So I kept my calm and prayed to get back safely.

After some awkward silences, he opted for us to leave and the drive back was ghostly quiet. Just as we approached the hotel, he pulled over and said, "I just want to fuck you."

I was dumbfounded, and I said, "What?"

He replied, "I wish you will give me an opportunity to fuck you."

I said, "No pastor, please don't talk like that. Surely this is an attack on you from the devil." Trying desperately to open the car door, I said, "Please don't let me be the reason you whole ministry which you have spent years building come into disrepute."

He calmly said, "No, it's not the devil. I really love you and really want you. Afterward, I will pray for forgiveness and lead us in the prayer of repentance. God knows how much I desire you."

He allowed me to open the car, and I got out and walked back to the hotel.

This man did not physically touch me, yet I felt dirty and violated. I couldn't believe this pastor who had preached so powerfully to his almost 1000 member congregation that seemed so spiritually on point was such a pervert. When I got back, I went straight to the shower and back to bed where I spent most of the night reflecting on some of the encounters I had with so-called men of God.

These experiences sent me into a place of deep distrust for men especially ones that name and claim spiritual authority. I became paranoid and sceptical. I began to build walls.

I knew it was important for me to be with someone who

shared my core values, but I was so broken that I found myself being many things, for some 15 years, namely:

The Convenient Alternative:

I went out one day and bumped into an old friend. He had matured like fine wine from when I had last seen him. We exchanged details and started to speak. It was evident that there was a mutual attraction. He pursued me hard. That felt good. I remember once we went out. He took me to an eye watering old villa Italian restaurant along the banks of the river Thames called The Elephant on the River. As I looked at him, I felt my ex-husband had reincarnated into this handsome, mixed-race dude. There was a hint of a control freak in the way he spoke. There was so much of his perspectives that reminded me of my ex. I literally got up in the middle of the meal and walked out.

He paid hastily and pursued me home. He apologised and promised to change. He wanted me at all cost and said he would go to the moon and back to make me happy. I consented to being his steady exclusive girlfriend thereafter. In the early stages, things went well, and I felt I was lucky to have found someone like him. This guy had weird doctrinal convictions, was clearly bipolar, and at times almost a mental basket case.

He once stood in front of the block of flats where he lived and tore his clothes when I refused to accept a bottle of perfume he had bought me after an argument. On another occasion, he threatened to jump over the balcony from the 13th floor of the building where he lived if I do not let him see what is inside my bag. Just total madness. He turned up one day at about 8 pm and offered to take me for a romantic moonlit drive. I gladly jumped in his car, and this guy drove all night with no destination or plan. He brought me back home, dog tired and sleep deprived at 4 am.

As time evolved, he became more and more emotionally unavailable. I found out that he was seeing other people. I became a self-trained and certified FBI and CIA agent. The more I hung with this guy, the more his insanity rubbed off on me. I began tracking his movements, checking his phone, parking outside his house to catch him with other women. Finally, one day he told me he was unavailable due to a DIY project he had undertaken for a friend of his.

In my gut, I knew he was lying. I withheld my number and called his phone one of the nights, and I could hear a lady talking in the background as he unsuccessfully tried to hush her. He then told me a series of lies to what had happened that night. On several other occasions, we had arguments that often involved other women. However, I was the go-to woman when he was stressed, broke, tired, or hungry. I decided to cut ties with this guy because clearly, I was an appendage and a convenient alternative.

The Experiment

Just before I went to the U.S., my brother Brian, who then lived in America, had my picture up on his wall. A Dominican friend of his once went to visit him and saw my photo. He apparently could not get over how beautiful I looked. So he got in touch with me in the UK, and we started to dialogue. I loved his voice and his accent and could not wait to see him in the flesh.

The day I drove into Minnesota, he was there waiting to welcome me. I was totally mashed up with the cross country driving we had needed to get there. So our exchange was pleasant but short.

Soon thereafter, we started dating. As time unfolded, I realised he was curious of what it would be like to date a girl of African descent. The whole relationship was like a major experiment. He had African friends who has exposed him to African food, which he absolutely loved, so I became a chef. He kept requesting I cook one thing after the other.

He was forever a student as that was how he had figured he would live legally in the U.S., so he basically enrolled in one course after another. Even though this guy was much older than I, we were never able to sit and have a constructive discussion on future plans or goals—he did not have any. I then became a counsellor, continuously encouraging him to set goals and how to go about meeting them.

After a while, a much older lady from the West Indies joined the church we both attended. I noticed they very quickly became uncomfortably close. I felt invincible, unwanted, taken for granted, undermined, and betrayed. Any time I questioned him on their relationship, he gave me the same answer: they had a lot more in common than we did, and she represents 'his familiar' so I should let them hang out.

This lady was married and had left her husband to further her studies. I was intuitively convinced they were sleeping together; although, he would vehemently deny it often calling curses on himself. Finally, the lady fell pregnant and her husband divorced her in absentia. The church insisted they get married. Our relationship effectively ended. They went on to have two children after which the lady cheated again with a man who was the husband of a dear friend of hers.

This resulted in their divorce. The guy has made numerous attempts to get back with me, sighting he made the biggest mistake of his life. Surely not for a woman who was only an experiment.

The Other Woman

So my cousins and I formed a group called the fun-loving forum. We decided come rain, come shine we should and will enjoy life. So we will spontaneously whip up parties or organise day trips when we will all hang out, play board games, eat out, or dance the night away.

One member of the group once brought his girlfriend along to one of out get together. She blended in like we had known her all our lives. In a matter of months, they got engaged and very soon thereafter they were getting married. We all got involved, quickly formed a wedding planning committee, and it was so beautiful. The day was lovely, and everything went to plan. As is typical in African parties in London, a lot of people gate crashed the wedding.

As I sat at the reception, tired from the days' activities, I saw this handsome stranger walk in. Our eyes locked, and the magic happened. I stood at a corner toward the back of the room, and he kept staring at me. One of my cousins observed the exchange of glances, and he said, "I think that guy is so into you." I began to blush.

After what seemed like an eternity, he finally came over and asked me to dance. I felt like I was dancing with the most eligible bachelor in the room. We talked as we danced, exchanged numbers, and he respectfully returned me to my seat afterward. Everyone noticed something was brewing and teased me no end!

The next morning, he called when I was getting ready for church. So I asked him, "Are you single and are you a Christian?"

He jokingly responded, "Yes Ma'am—on both counts your highness." We quickly started dating, and I had not had this much fun in ages. He said he was looking to relocate to a more vibrant church and without much debate, quickly became a member in our church. We had a great friendship and spent endless hours on the phone talking. We would meet at car parks, blast loud music from our cars, and dance under the stars like two little kids. We both just loved having fun and clicked so much.

As time went by, he explained to me that he had two kids. However, he claimed the younger one was not his biological kid and that his ex-wife had had an affair, which had led to their divorce. Nonetheless, he decided to father the innocent child. Without explaining, he would publicly acknowledge him, but he had quietly put his wife away for her infidelity. A month after we met, he came over to visit with a massive bouquet of flowers. He knelt down and made a little speech thanking me for letting him into my life. He was such a romantic.

Once we were on the phone chatting, and I broke my nail. It hurt so much, I started to cry. He got in his car, while we were still talking and drove all the way to my house. Suddenly, I heard my doorbell, so I put him on hold, ran downstairs, and low and behold, he was right there.

"Baby, I came by to kiss your nail better." He held me affectionately, had a look at my broken nail, kissed it better, and left. I honestly thought this guy had fallen right out of Heaven, and I was totally magnetized to him. Word got around my mum's circle that I was dating him, and an aunt of mine who knew of him called my mum and advised my mum to tell me to dump him as he was not honest with me as he was in fact married. I asked him if there was anything I needed to know, and of course, he said nothing. A couple of weeks of him visiting me for the first time, he turned up at my home and proposed to me.

I turned him down because frankly, while I had enjoyed all the attention, I did not know him! I told him, "I haven't met anyone in your life or your family, so really I think it is a little premature." We continued seeing each other, and the bond we had was amazing. We shared love for music and movies, went on endless dates, sampled various restaurants, and had a whole lot of fun. He was such a breath of fresh air. He had the warmest hugs and the brightest, most assuring smile.

One morning while I was getting ready for work, my home phone rang. I contemplated picking it or not as a long conversation would have definitely made me late for work. I decided to pick it up and to advise the caller of a later call. To my horror, it was his wife! She calmly introduced herself and said that she had been made to understand that I am dating her husband, and she was advising me to leave him alone as they had a young family.

I was absolutely dumbfounded. I found it hard to digest what I was hearing. I told her I was off to work, but I would like to meet her. So we scheduled a meeting for the weekend.

I drove to the location we had agreed to meet and got there a little earlier than planned. At 10am on the dot, I saw this lady walk into the restaurant with two young kids who look exactly like their father. My heart sank!

So we exchanged pleasantries and got to the heart of the matter after setting down the kids in high chairs over breakfast. Firstly, I apologised profusely for dating her husband and explained I did not know that he was married. I explained his sob story about her having an affair, and she turned to the younger one and said, "Having now seen this baby, does he look like someone else's kid?" I was so torn apart that I was an instrument in the hand of the enemy that could possibly destroy a family.

I asked how come he lived on his own. She then explained that their house had subsidence, and they had moved out, mutually agreeing to live apart until the house was repaired. I apologised and assured her she will no longer have to worry about him cheating with me. From that moment, it was over.

I left the restaurant, called him, and ended the relationship. Again, I felt betrayed, disappointed, and totally let down. I told him I had just had breakfast with his family, and I never wanted to hear from him again. There are two questions I would've love to have asked him, which to this day I have no answers. Why would you want to risk losing such a beautiful family over an affair? And the second one was: Why? Why did you come into my life, and lie so much and even faked a proposal?

Why? I never got my answers, and even though I have crossed paths with this guy on occasion, things have been so frosty that we have never been able to sit and talk. I realised I was simply 'the other woman.' I saw them recently, and this couple are still very much married. So glad that their marriage did not end. I was clearly just the other woman.

The Hopeful One

Once an old friend of mine asked me to help him with some IT problems he was having. So I made an appointment and drove across town to go have a look at my friend's desktop. I was greeted at the door by a dark, well-built, average looking man. He smiled charmingly and let me in. As I fixed my friend's machine, we had a chit chat, and he let me into the understanding that he was holidaying in London, and he would like me to take him to the Annual Notting Hill Carnival. I had not been to the carnival in ages, and I was not prepared to go. So I politely declined. Nonetheless, we exchange numbers and kept in touch.

He went back to Hull where he was based, and we kept in touch. He was eight years younger than me, yet I had always felt age was a number. So I continued to encourage his advances. We became great friends, and as a medical doctor, I found him extremely intelligent, and we could converse for hours. Once I was based out of Manchester for work, so I'd spend weekends at home in London while the working week in Manchester. He called me one day that he would like to visit. We scheduled a weekend that I was not in London, and I prepared to host him. He turned up mid-afternoon on the Saturday, and I was equally prepared to host him.

I cooked a feast. We sat down to a lovely and delightful meal. We chatted and laughed late into the evening. This was the 2nd time I was meeting this guy, and he made an impression on me. So as night approached, I wondered why he made no moves to start heading back since he had a 3 to 4-hour return journey, and there was no expectation that he was spending the weekend. At some point, he insinuated that he was tired, and if I do not mind, he will love to sleep over. I had a guest airbed, so I consented. I got the airbed pumped up downstairs and went upstairs to bed. He did not look impressed at all. At about 2am, I had some movements in my room. He had crawled upstairs and was making his way into my bed. I put on my bedside lamp, and I saw this guy who I had graciously hosted standing stark naked in my room. I let out a scream so loud, I wonder how far my voice went. He was absolutely embarrassed and started begging that all he wants to do is make love to me. I was horrified. I felt so scared. I screamed as I asked him to just leave my room and get dressed. This 6'4 guy could have raped me in my own home. He left my room and returned at about 4am, saying that he was ready to leave. I saw him off at the door. Before he left, he took time to verbally insult me. He told me I should have been grateful that a man of his standing would have considered me—a divorcee with a child. He asked me if I thought he was foolish enough to pursue me for a long-term relationship. In his anger, he blurted out that if indeed we had ended up in a relationship, he would have got his immigration papers and dumped me like a hot potato. I then realised I was the foolish one.

I laid in bed for a long time after he had left, thinking about the poor calibre of men we had left in our generation. I felt a deep sadness in my soul. As I laid in my bed, tears rolled down my eyes. The words he spoke were so hurtful. I found it hard to believe what had just happened. What happened to chivalry? Where were the boys who had been raised to respect and honour women? I dried my tears, got up, and got ready for work. The whole day, my mind was doing gymnastics—wondering if there were any real men in our generation. Needless to say, I never saw or heard from him again. Why I ever hoped that this guy was worth my while was beyond me in hindsight.

The Believer Against All Odds

So when I was in my teens, I had met a guy with whom I really clicked. We were two crazy kids. Sometimes when I am tired, he would carry me on his back. We took lots of sunset walks along the beach when time permitted and had so much fun together. He was in medical school, while I was still in high school. He was a bunch of brains, and his intelligence intrigued me. We got on like house on fire and became really great friends. So when I left for the UK, he left for the U.S., and we never set eyes on each other or spoke in very many years. Like any childhood friend, he did cross my mind, and I often wondered what had become of him, if he was happy with life's curveballs and what he looked like and so on.

After a few years of living with me especially after Adiel had gone to school, Mum found out that she had some time on her hands, and she decided to fill her week with various activities. She found a local church that had some mid-week meetings, joined an exercise club with people her age, and made a healthy social life. One of the days after she had attended a service, she come home and told me of an exceptionally beautiful young lady who was very kind and courteous. Mum thought that she might be of Jamaican decent but wasn't sure. Finally, I got to meet this lady and realised she was the sister of the guy I had met a number of years ago. I was so happy to be connected to her and in that sense to be reconnected to my old crazy friend. I really desired to know how life had treated him, but she said very little. A year later, she was getting married, and I asked if her brother was attending. She was unsure as he had made no firm commitments. It was a beautiful and very big wedding ceremony. The church was filled to capacity and thankfully a very warm day for the month of March.

I came out of the church and hung out with a group of friends, talking and laughing. I laughed characteristically at a joke that was shared, and suddenly, I heard someone behind me say, "Avril? I know that laugh!" I turned around and saw my childhood friend who had kept a recording of my voice in his head for over 20 years. I ran into his arms. It was such a joyous reunion. For the next 30 minutes, we were locked in conversation.

We exchanged details and decided we will meet again before he returns to the U.S. It was a weekend trip as he had flown in to surprise his sister. He was due to fly back on the Monday morning. On Sunday, my phone rang, and he said he was feeling quite jetlagged, and due to the festivities the day before, if I do not mind, can he come finish sleeping on my couch so we can have a conversation as best we could with the limited energy he had.

I advised him to sleep at home and come by in the evening. At about 7:30pm, my doorbell rang, and to my delight, he was there, looking much more rested than he had sounded. I was so bowled over and honoured that he would chose to spend time with me. I was cooking my son's dinner to freeze for the week, and he sat with me in the kitchen, spontaneously helping were he could. After about 30 minutes, we settled in the living room and started catching up properly.

So much time had elapsed, and there was so much to catch up on. Our craziness was rekindled in a flash. We talked and laughed so much, my cheeks hurt. We blinked, and it was almost 3am. Time had flown, and we hadn't noticed. He had not packed his things, so he decided to leave. Before we parted ways, he gave me a lingering hug. I liked this guy. He got safely back to Atlanta, and as soon as the plane touched down, he texted me, and we started what ended up being a 3-hour dialogue. In the next 5 weeks, we spoke nonstop.

The conversations got longer and longer and juicier and juicier. We were inseparably communicating. I slowly started to fall for this guy. I found his being in my life a breath of fresh air. He was not intimidated by me in anyway. Where other men had tried to place limitations on me, he pushed me to excel and created a safe space for me to be myself. He was a lot of fun to be around and to have in my life. Finally, one day, the conversations focused on 'us.' He claimed that I was his ideal woman and that I had everything he was looking for in a woman; however, he was too wounded, broken, and hurt from his broken marriage to ever marry again. For the life of me, I don't know why this did not sink in.

For some bizarre reason, I believed my being in this guy's life would change that conviction. It was too good to be true. He was not your regular heart throb. He was not very tall, stocky, and not the most handsome guy around yet he tickled my heart, and he did something to my brain I had not experienced in a long time. I was intellectually stimulated. After about a year, things got steamier between us. He brought out the best in me. We did not see often but spoke daily, sometimes several times a day. On one occasion, he flew into the UK to surprise me for a weekend and told all his cousins to meet mine if they wanted to see me. I whipped up a BBQ that turned into a party.

It was spontaneous, but it was beautiful and memorable. This guy had a magic about him. The sticking point though, was that every time the conversation went to commitment, he would reiterate that while I was everything he desires in a woman, he never wants to get married again in this life. I was very much the 'woman' in his life as time as time unfolded. We spoke first thing every morning his time, which was around lunch time my time, and it was amazing how much we bonded. It took three years and many tears to realise I had met a perfect match, yet he was totally unavailable. It was evident he loved me, and I did everything I could to make him see that I would make the perfect wife if he could just allow his heart to love again, but his brokenness and fear did not permit him.

He had a confidential conversation with his brother that was overheard by his wife with whom I was quite close. She sat me down and explained to me that I needed to find a way to detangle myself from this guy and move on. I remember tearfully sending him a long text, opening my heart and articulating my disappointment at the realisation that our story must pause because fundamentally we want different things out of love and life. I had loved a man against all odds to my disappointment.

The Long Sufferer

So I took a break from dating for a while to catch my breath. At this point, I was confused and emotionally drained. I just concluded that maybe this love thing was beyond my reach. I decided I wanted to focus on me and understand who Avril really was and what Avril really wanted. Other areas in my life were blossoming, and I simply did not understand how to navigate my way into the heart of a man.

I decided to attend a few relationship and singles conferences. I hated them completely. I just felt being single was so awkward, and there were always married people trying to convince the singles that there was something they needed to learn or that there was a 'level of singleness' that needed to be achieved that had not being achieved hence why people are still single. I really found some of the single conferences disturbing.

I began to realise also that there was a stigma attached to being single and moreso after divorce especially. It was almost always assumed that it was your fault that you cannot keep your marriage. I decided to stop hanging out at these damning conferences and to carve out a path to love myself. I bought books that spoke to my self-worth and value and listened to videos that built me up. For over a year, I did not date. I made sure that I established what I needed in a man and weed out anything that was a distraction.

One day, I was invited to a christening party. I had been friends with the baby's dad from University and back in the day whenever we got together, it is usually madness and mayhem. The party was wild! We danced and kept the neighbours awake all night long and just vegetated in be the next day. The christening party was no different.

He called me to thank me and mentioned that a personal friend of his had taken a fancy to me. I was so focussed on the reunion that I did not even realise that there was someone else who was not part of our study year that was present. He convinced me that his friend was cool, and he could vouch for him and maybe, just maybe, he might be the one. So I agreed for my number to be passed on.

Within a couple of hours, I had a call from an unfamiliar number on my phone. I had spent the day recovering from the party, and I answered the phone quite sluggishly. "Hey this is Akin. We haven't met formerly, but I saw you yesterday, and I feel so lucky that you agreed to get your number passed on to me."

"Ah, you are the bloke Blake mentioned, uh?" I responded still sounding sleepy.

"Yes, yes," he said eagerly. "Actually, you sound quite tired. Why don't you save my number and give me a bell when you have recovered from yesterday's shenanigans?"

I sat up in bed and said, "No, no, I have spent all day sleeping. Let's chat, just give me a few minutes to wash my face, and we can talk."

Frankly, this guy's voice was so rich and so deep, it was hard to stop talking with him. That conversation ended up being 4 hours. We gelled effortlessly and laughed a lot in the process. It was refreshing and delightful. During the conversation, we learnt we lived 3 hours apart, and it would be near impossible with our various schedules to meet regularly. We kept in touch and had many marathon conversations over a 2-year period. Somehow, it was never mutually convenient for us to meet.

I realised I had grown to be really fond of this guy and vice versa. He came across honest, transparent, accountable, God-fearing, lovable, and open. Above all, he was funny and never ceased to make me laugh.

We had a mutual friend, Al, who tried on many an occasion to engineer a meeting between us. On a cold October day, one of my godmothers was celebrating her birthday. She formed a team of 6 helpers to ensure things ran smoothly from refilling the food supply to clearing the tables. I was responsible to ensure that the kitchen was kept clutter free and after she had cut her birthday cake, that the cake was boxed up in little cubes.

As is the tradition among young people in London, parties get gate crashed. The mutual friend Akin and I had called me during the week and casually asked what I will be up to during the weekend for my godmother's birthday celebration. I mentioned the upcoming birthday party. I told him that if he did not have anything going, he could drop by. He took the opportunity and liberty to invite Akin to the do. About a couple of hours into the event, Al found me and casually asked me to go outside and meet someone.

It was so cold and crisp and even though I was hard at work in the kitchen and not necessarily cold there, I was quite reluctant to go out. After much persuasion, I conceded. To my amazement, Akin stood there. I was speechless. I just wrapped my hands around his neck and hugged him super tight. I then held his hands and walked into the party introducing him to people as we went in. I went to my mum and introduced him. My mum was delighted to finally meet the mystery guy who I had spent hours on the phone with.

Then we took to the dance floor. We spent the next three hours dancing non-stop. It was crazy and intense. Surely to my knowledge I had never met this guy, yet the physical connection I felt in those 3 hours was at a different level. We chatted like two birds and just laughed the night away. I totally forgot my commitment to help. At one point, an announcement had to be made over the PA system for me to get to my designated job. I sneaked out again and re-joined him on the dance floor. It was clear that there was a strong physical and emotional attraction between Akin and I. Finally, the party came to an end. I bade him farewell and just before he left he whispered in my ear "call you tomorrow at 8pm."

8pm the following day, sharp on the dot, my phone rang. I jolted and picked it up. I was so excited to hear his brassy baritone voice again. We chatted till 4am.

As a family, we travelled to Andalucia in Spain the Monday after the party, where we had planned to spend the week for Adiel's half term. After the 3rd day on holiday, I woke up at about 3am, and my whole system was burning with love. I had never experienced anything like this. It was like my heart was on fire. It is hard to explain. I knew my soul had fallen for Akin.

Somehow, we had never kissed nor met for 2 years. Yet for the first time, I knew I was in love. I woke up my mum and asked her if she could tell me what it felt like when a woman is in love. My mum open one eye and very drowsily said, "What time is it Avril?"

"Almost 4 in the morning," I replied.

She shut the one eye and muttered, "Please darling let's talk about love in the morning, shall we?"

I found it hard to drop back to sleep. I could not understand what was happening to me. There was a warm and a deep longing to belong to Akin and be on his team.

Finally, it was daybreak, and my mum and I settled into a typical Spanish breakfast—alfresco style. As we discussed my discovery of this 'in love' experience, my phone rang and it was Akin on the line. I excused myself from breakfast and went on to have the conversation indoors as we had not spoken since I left the UK. I listened keenly as Akin explained to me that exactly what was happening to me was what was happening to him. He had known what is was like to have lusted after a woman and what it was like to have had casual relationships.

Yet for the first time in his life he felt he had fallen in love in a 'pure' way. What was happening to us was so mutual and amazing and somewhat beyond our understanding.

We returned to the UK, and I decided that for the first time I was going to go see Akin physically to establish if the feelings I had were just a fleeting sensation or something deeper. I drove for 3 hours, praying all the way. Finally, I entered the midlands. It was magical. I was so excited. I called Akin and told him I was in his neck of the woods. He could not believe his ears. He directed me to his bachelor's pad. I drove through the picturesque town of Worcester and got to his place. He received me at the door with a warm hug. As we entered his home, he shuffled things around. It was obvious that he wasn't expecting anyone. He apologised that he had no food and ordered some Chinese take away. We sat down and looked into each other's eyes as we spoke—catching up from where we left off while I was on holiday. He kept pinching himself, not believing I was right in front of him! It was amazing how much I felt I had shifted emotionally to loving this guy. The powerful and interesting thing is how strongly we felt mutually for each other.

The food arrived, and he did his best to create some romance by lighting a few candles as we dined. I was just happy to be with him, and I did not want the moment to end. Finally, we finished eating and I decided to leave. He stood up and deliberately invaded my personal space as he embraced me. For the first time in two years since I met this guy, we shared a kiss.

It was magical and unbelievable. *Surely, finally, I have met 'the one,'* I thought. I hastily left for a three-hour drive back to London. There was not moment when my mind was blank. It was like I had had a sneak preview into Heaven. I was on cloud nine. I got home close to midnight. We spoke for a short while, and I dropped off to sleep. Without it being formerly discussed, we started an exclusive relationship.

I felt so 'at home' with Akin, but very quickly, I realised he lacked the emotional wholeness that one needs to possess to have a long-term relationship. I decided that come hell or high water, I will hang in there and allow him to go through his personal metamorphosis. He exhibited great insecurities and the un-forgiveness he had for his ex-wife manifested itself in so many strange ways. At some point, he began to feel that he was still in love with his ex. In spite of all these red flags, I held on to our seeming supernatural encounter and held on for dear life.

Our relationship was nothing short of a rollercoaster. How and why I was so long suffering remains a mystery to me. We developed a way to spice up our relationship by playing a game to introduce each other to something or somewhere either of us were unfamiliar with or had not been before, once a month. In one such trip, Akin took me to Malta for a long weekend, and while there, he proposed to me. It was so unexpected yet so sweet.

He had told both my mum and his, and I was bowled over. Akin had asked me to pack a lovely dinner outfit and that we will be going out for a nice meal somewhere special. The morning of the day before we left, he came to my room and woke me up, and not being a morning person, I was quite irritated. He sat on the bed and took my hand. In a very sweet voice, he said, "Do you actually see yourself growing old with me?"

I rolled my eyes and said, "Akin, couldn't you have asked me that at midday when I am fully awake?" He apologised and reaffirmed his love for me. He was being so sweet, it was hard not to be suspicious; however, we were on a romantic break, so I just let it slip by. We later took a beach front walk and spoke of the life we would live as a family and just looked into our future. The whole day just felt so super special.

In the evening, we were both dressed to the nines and went for the mysterious dinner date he had arranged at the 'secret location.' We took a short walk to the pier on the beach and were greeted by waiters with a bunch of flowers. *How nice!* I thought as we were ushered to our seat. The sun was setting as we tucked into a delightful meal. It was perfect, and then desert was served and concealed in the heart shaped fruit concoction was a beautiful ring! I was shocked and dumbfounded, and the joy that filled my heart was indescribable.

Akin went down on one knee. He made a speech about I have made him happier than he had ever imagined possible, and he would want to give me an opportunity to bring me happiness every day thereafter and would like an opportunity to be my husband. I asked him very calmly to sit down as all eyes were on us. I could hear gasps throughout the restaurant. I said, "Akin, I know we have been going out for two years, and I am sure you know where I stand, but please do not ever cheat on me or hit me."

"I promise," he whispered.

"Now, my knight in shining armour, you can ask me again" I replied.

He knelt down again, cleared his throat as if to draw attention to himself again and asked with boldness and confidence, "Avril, the queen of my heart and centre of my world, will you be my wife?"

I smiled and nodded vigorously as tears filled my eyes, and with all the energy I could muster in that moment, I said, "Yes!" I stretched my hand, and he placed the ring on it, and the whole restaurant erupted with cheers and whistles.

I couldn't wait to get back to the hotel to call my mum. I just felt as if I was walking on clouds. We called his mum, and to my surprise, she blurted out, "Congrats! I am so happy for you."

I look at Akin, and he had a big grin on his face. His mum was over the moon and doubly delighted that I was soon going to be a part of their family officially.

We called my mum, and all she asked was, "How did it go? So very happy for you my baby."

We spent the night discussing where we will tie the knot and whether we will have a quiet or huge ceremony. After much deliberation, we agreed we will have a traditional engagement ceremony in London (where most of my family members are), and we will have our wedding in Barbados (where most of his family members were). I had never really thought highly of beach weddings, and I certainly did not want sand in my feet on my wedding day. We made a decision to take a holiday to Barbados to explore what we could practically achieve with our budget.

A few months after the proposal in Malta, we flew out to Barbados. His mum booked us with a wedding planner, and she discuss some alternatives with us. It was an exciting time, and I got to experience Barbados culturally with the advantage of Akin's parents being locals. The cuisine was different and generally spicier but ever so flavoursome. We had lunch and dinner dates with his extended family, and I thought I would explode from overeating. I was very, very, very warmly received.

We had a few meetings with the wedding planner, and things were taking shape nicely. However, I realised that Akin was surprisingly overly possessive and extremely jealous of anyone that gave me any attention—even his own relatives. This is not a side I had seen of him before. At a point, he grabbed my phone when I went to have a shower and sent a message to one of my pastors that was checking up on me.

He wrote the message as if it was from me asking him not to ever contact me again. When I came back and realised what he had done, I lost it. He threatened to jump over a cliff not far from their house as he was convinced I was having an affair with the pastor. His behaviour was erratic and extremely bizarre and got me thinking whether this guy was stable enough to hold down a marriage. It recollected a few days earlier when we went to hang out at a place called St. Lawrence gap.

He was jealous that he felt other men were looking at me. After some time, less than an hour, he asked that we leave as "he wasn't feeling the place." We went home and played board games. To add insult to injury, one day we were in his parent's living room, and he sat on the floor leaning against the couch that I was on as he checked his mail. As he loaded his mail, I could hear several instant message bleeps on his yahoo messenger. I leaned over and ask who that was. He quickly closed the chat window and said he didn't know.

I got curious, my heart sank. In my gut, I knew Akin was seeing someone else. His response sparked off a massive argument. In our relationship, we had established total transparency. We had keys to each other's homes, access to each other's mail, knew each other's cash card pin numbers, and was listed on each other's car insurance. For the life of me, I could not understand why Akin chose to lie to me. Why now? We were planning on becoming man and wife, and for the first time in what was now 4 years after we met, he was sowing seeds of doubt in my heart. I purposed at this point that I would discontinue wedding arrangements until I establish with clarity what was going on. I refused to commit to any firm plans for our wedding or part with money in the way of any deposits. The rest of our time in Barbados was laced with arguments that left me with a deep sense of uncertainty and insecurity.

When we got back to the UK, his best friend's wife called me and told me that she felt she needed to share something with me, knowing that I was away planning my wedding.

"Akin had been seeing a girl locally, and she has no idea that you exist or that he is about to get married," she told me. She was unaware of what had transpired when we were in Barbados and just felt she wanted to protect me from eminent heartache.

I could feel the walls of my castle crashing down. I asked her for the number of the girl in question and proceeded to call her. I calmly introduced myself and apologised for interrupting her day. I explained that I was Akin's fiancée, and I wanted to extend a hand of friendship to her knowing that she was already friends with my husband to be. She started to hyperventilate, and I had to ask her several times if she was okay. She explained to me that they were not friends but lovers and that they had actually had an intimate relationship for over 6 months.

Akin had even promised her they will get married and all he was requesting was for her to exercise some patience as he works out a few things in his life. The betrayal I felt was like the stabbing of multiple knives simultaneously. I asked her not to worry and that she could have him because I certainly didn't. I hastily ended the call and cried loudly so hard and so long. It felt like I was going through a divorce all over again. I felt broken, deceived, violated, stupid, unwanted, unworthy of true love, and very deeply hurt.

Before I hung up, she asked me for my email as she wanted to send me evidence of their relationship. Nothing could have prepared me for what my eyes saw when I finally accessed my mail. Their relationship was explicitly sexual, and they had even sent nude pictures to each other. I needed no further explanation. I called Akin, told him I had found out he was cheating and asked him where I would leave the things he had at my house and if he could kindly return any property of mine in his possession.

"Avril," he protested, "you cannot do this. How can you throw away 4 years of our lives together just like that? It's not what you think. I really need an opportunity to explain myself. There was nothing to it. It was just sex, casual sex. I don't love her. Never had, never will!"

I couldn't believe my ears. I lit the barbeque and took every gift and anything Akin had given me over the 4 years and burnt it all. The abrupt end of our relationship sparked off a whole year of very intense grief. I could not contain the pain my heart went through. I would often go to church and cry the whole way through the service. I would sit in public and just thinking about the loss of the relationship and losing Akin, would cause me to start balling uncontrollably. I was a complete mess. I went through self-doubt and questioned how I could not have seen this coming.

How could I have been such a poor judge of character? On one occasion after a week of crying and not eating much, I went to Adiel's parent teacher meeting, and as the teacher spoke to me, I felt my head going in circles, and the next thing I knew, I was in hospital. I had passed out. How after a divorce could I have allowed another human being to hurt me so deeply? It took me a whole year to rationalise my thoughts and to accept that I cannot control what other people do, but I can control how I react to life's vicissitudes. I can to own my own happiness and found my safe place again.

Soon after my divorce was finalised, I made a vow that I would save myself again for my next husband, and I would protect my heart from being scarred in the process of waiting. In the months that I processed the breakup of my engagement with Akin, I began to revisit those commitments and resolved to get to that place again. I felt there were life lessons I had failed to learn, and I could not understand why I attracted people that hurt me brutally or clearly did not value who I was.

I decided to hold off dating for a while and find myself in a way that will not be defined by a relationship or another person. I felt that the bad experiences that I had encountered emotionally were eating away at the beautiful person I was internally. I felt my ability to love unreservedly with reckless abandon and to, more importantly, receive love freely, was being stifled. So I decided on embarking on a journey to heal before I deal again.

CLOSURE

Here I was, years after my divorce and multiple relationships that had not worked, I was like an injured soldier in a battle. Was I saved and practising my faith? Certainly! However, I was a broken woman looking for love in all the wrong places. I really did not know what to do with my heart. I had this strong desire to love and be loved just the way my soul desired, but somehow, I just couldn't break through in that aspect of my life.

Some fifteen years had elapsed after my divorce. Apart from the turbulence I had faced in attracting the wrong guys, I had done very well in all other areas of my life. God had made a way for us as a family. Mum had settled well into life in the UK again, and we got on well. Adiel had gone through private education and was doing extremely well with clarity about what line of work he desires pursue after formal education. I had passed every qualifying exam and achieved fellowship in my field of work after emerging with a distinction from my master's degree. I was in ministry serving in the church.

At a point, I concluded that maybe I am just one of those people who may never marry. I went on to define the life I wanted, found things that brought me fulfilment and got on with life. I started travelling widely. However, I couldn't escape the nudging of my heart to not give up on love. The open wound and the insecurity of the lack of love in my life manifested itself in several ways. Even though on the outside I seemed to be doing so well, I suffered from anxiety and insomnia. I would heavily criticise people who were doing their best to make their relationships work because deep down I thought they were wasting their time.

I was a seasoned an established driver that had driven all over the country for work yet for no apparent reason I started to feel uneasy and scared while driving. I couldn't understand it. I would go to the garage and have my breaks checked frequently. I just had a feeling in my gut that something bad was going to happen to me.

One day, just as I had thought, a lorry driver tried to overtake me on the passenger side of my car and entered ahead of me prematurely. He grazed my car with me in it dragging it along the central reservation of a dual carriageway and dragged me some 50 meters before realising it had hit me.

I was glad to still be alive when he stopped as he had cleaned the whole passenger side of the car. The driver fell to the ground, held his head, and cried because my car looked like a metal ball, and he thought he had killed me. The delayed shocked registered in my subconscious some 20 minutes later.

I went into deep shock. I started to bleed, I started to vomit and went completely numb. I was rescued home by the emergency services and my life changed.

I started having nightmares. I was scared to get out of the house. Whenever I got in a car, if it went fast, on getting to my destination, I would need to step out and vomit. I bled for 2 weeks in the middle of my menstrual cycle. My whole life seemed to have been turned upside down. I took time off work as I went virtually speechless. Most times when my mum spoke to me, all I could do in response was nod. I had to stop driving. I felt like I had lost my independence. I had to rely on others for basic things like help with moving around. I did not feel safe being in a bus or on the train alone. It took me a while to have any semblance of normality in my life.

My insurers tried to reach the company of the driver that had hit my car, and they claimed he was nowhere to be found. They had to take legal action to get the company to accept liability. The insomnia intensified.

I went to see my GP who recommended I try some herbal sleep aids as I was too young to be put on sleeping tablets, as they generally have addictive side effects. I started drinking herbal Nytol and that improved my sleep quality a whole lot. However, the nightmares continued. I went to see my GP again, and he recommended that I go for an assessment at Harley Street to establish what was going on.

I went on to Harley Street for a mental health assessment. At my consultation, I was asked to fill out a form that had what seemed to me like a whole lot of irrelevant questions, about my childhood, family life etc. etc. Anyway after a chat with the consultant, I was asked to go into another room and had some things wired to my head and my pulses. I was then asked a series of questions regarding the accident and other events that were traumatic to me as a child.

After the consultation, I returned to the consultant's office, and he reviewed the results. He sat me down and explained I was dealing with Post Traumatic Stress Disorder

(PTSD). He said, "Actually, your results are like that of a soldier who has been to war and seen his comrades die. I cannot stress how important it is for you to have a lot of self-care. You need help, and I would recommend to your GP that you have some Cognitive Behavioural Therapy (CBT) sessions, and we can review thereafter."

I returned to my GP, and I was referred to a few NHS therapists for CBT sessions. I turned up at the first lady's house and was ushered into her therapy room that had some strange incense burning and some very bizzare instrumental music that sounded like a chant from a cult. She reviewed the notes she had in the referral from the GP and went on to tell me she was a certified psychotherapist and the range of alternative medical help she can give me.

I felt very uncomfortable in her surroundings and made up my mind that when I leave, I will not return. She said, "In your case, I reckon the best thing for you may not be CBT but hypnosis. I can get you hypnotized and erase the memory of the accident." I wasn't sure of what hypnosis entailed, but there was something about this woman that I did not trust. When I asked her what hypnosis entailed, she said, "I will put you to sleep somewhat and take over your will and whatever I suggest to you at that point becomes your reality." That was it for me! I told her I did not fancy handing over my will to another person. We concluded the session and decided that she might not be the therapist to help me. I returned to my GP and was referred to another therapist.

I turned up at her house, and it had several dogs and cats running wild. It was like the scene out of a horror movie. She ushered me into her therapy room, and we settled down. She seemed okay and very different from the former lady I had met. However, I don't think she 'got' me. I felt detached and somewhat of a statistic to her. After a few sessions, I did not feel I was making much progress. She asked me to find a dot, focus on it and think good thoughts towards it. Every time I feel anxious, I must focus on the dot and recollect my good thoughts.

I thought this was too abstract for me along with the other mental exercises I did. So I decided to quit. A few weeks later, I was having a chat with my best friend Emma, and I discussed my failed therapy sessions with her. I was still dependent on the herbal tablets for a good night's sleep, and I felt I still needed therapy. She suggested someone she knew who ran a busy practice in East Grinstead and highly recommended him. That was a bit far for me, but I willing to do whatever it took to get the help I felt I needed, so I called the therapist.

He was a white, middle-aged man who sounded very nice and very willing to help. I explained how I felt about the other therapists, and he encouraged me to do some sessions with him so we can see how I get on.

I made my trip to East Grinstead and walked to his office. I noticed that psychologically, it felt better that I was meeting him in a more formal setting that at home. The office was clean, sparsely furnished, and the atmosphere felt quite pleasant. He was empathetic and promised to help me recover from the nightmare I was living. He did a similar assessment to the one I had had with the consultant, and I felt very much as ease with him.

For the first time, he helped me understand that my life although gloriously successful to the on-looker, I had suffered from numerous traumatic experiences. My therapy with this man lasted 2 solid years of weekly sessions, and we dealt with everything. I went right to root. My sessions were deep but necessary if I was to be whole again.

When I was four years old, my parents left us and went out for a party. The babysitter was a man they knew. Just around that time, there was a case of a young family friend raping a young girl, so to avoid a similar incident, they decided to lock me in their room. I woke up in the middle of the night in pitch darkness, needing the bathroom. I wet myself and screamed until my voice was gone. I fruitlessly tried to open the door, but I couldn't. I couldn't reach for the light switch.

I had only made it to the door because there was little ray of light from the street lamp that came through the curtain. The babysitter tried to calm me down to no avail. The neighbours heard me screaming and got in touch with my parents, and they returned. Although I couldn't fully recollect the details, my mum told me once that when they came back, I was so worked up I was shaking for over thirty minutes. Little did I know this was the first episode of trauma in my life.

The therapist teased out the painful situations that I had lived through. Recollecting my friend Rebecca who had drowned. I cried for 1 hour in therapy. It was the first time, I cried for her and about her death. We dealt with my father passing. I wept like a baby. Akpon did not like the bond I had with my father and often regarded my attachment to him idolatrous.

The therapist gave me reason, room and permission to grieve properly and find the closure I needed. Interestingly, while I was in therapy Leo, my first ever boyfriend, died. I got never got to meet with him after I left Freetown and never had an opportunity to speak with him. I had a call from an old friend, and I was told he passed away. It was surreal, I had not seen or heard from him in ages, yet I suddenly felt an emptiness. My therapy helped me grieve his loss and release him back to God. We addressed the trauma and stigma of going through a divorce, the psychological complications of being a single parent.

We spoke about the numerous failed relationships and realised I was attracting the wrong kind of men into my life because fundamentally although I am a very beautiful woman, I needed to re-write the perception I had of myself in line with who God says I am. Somewhere along the line, life experiences had taken a toll on my self-worth.

Like me, the therapist was a practising Christian. So, he understood how my life choices centred on my faith. I explained my cultural biases, and he helped me navigate my way out of shame and guilt and stigma that I was carrying as a divorcee. He helped me with dealing with the root of fear in my life and how it was threatening to take over my existence.

I realised that by the time I went into therapy with him I was fearful, anxious and uncertain of what love was. We started to deal with the spirit of fear. I learnt that perfect love casts out fear and faith is the opposite of fear. So I needed to stretch my faith to receive the love of God and allow it to penetrate my walls.

We worked as a team to deal with the enemies that plagued my mental health. I was living day by day with lies I had told myself, feeling unlovable, unwanted, unloved, inadequate, uncertain, and unworthy of love. I realised that we are raised to do life, trained in church to pray, worship and walk by faith, but the realm of emotional healing is one that is often overlooked. Mental health is somewhat taboo.

Breakthrough

My therapist told me the easiest way of changing my narrative is to change the way I think. My thoughts will shape my words and my words will create the world I will live in. I needed to start seeing myself the way God sees me ad allowing the Word of God—the Bible which is life to do what it does best—to transform my life. The life experiences I lived out were a reflection of my convictions. I went through a period of transformation with what I now fondly refer to my "I AM declarations". I remember when I was emerging from my divorce and my pastor would call me and pray over me. My spirit heard the words and because I allowed the words he spoke that were right out of the Bible to transform my world. My reality became the change he spoke into me.

I recited my "I AM declarations for months. Slowly and surely, I experienced healing, meaning and clarity. I found out that without being able to pinpoint the moment, there was a wholeness about the way I saw and felt about myself. I realised I did not need the affirmation of a man. I KNEW in my gut the value I now placed on myself was not dependent on some external influence. Another person's opinion no longer became my obligation.

My breakthrough was anchored in facing my pain, acknowledging it, but not letting my brokenness define me. I was empowered to soar, because all I was and all I was going to become was centred on my faith being anchored in God.

I realised that I was in myself inadequate, but with God I could truly do all things and be everything he purposed for me to be and do.

I was empowered and equipped to live my best life. I closed my therapy sessions knowing I was transformed and ready for my next season.

TRANSFORMATION

Janet put her hand up as if she was in a class. "I need the bathroom." Avril looked at the jug of the ginger-spiced lemonade they had been drinking all evening. It is empty. It's nearly midnight, over 3 hours from the beginning of her story.

"I knew you had something powerful to share Avril" Rosa remarked. "I remember I was working away when you told me you needed to go through therapy to start driving again. I am so glad you did. Your story has touched me in a way that's hard to explain. As you know, I have had my fair share of issues. This is going to help me make better choices."

"Don't continue without me!" Janet shouts from the bathroom.

Avril and Rosa burst out laughing. "Come on now, what's talking you so long?" Rosa asked.

"I will be out in a jiffy." Janet replied.

"Let me top up our lemonade" Avril said, turning to Rosa. "Girl, when life leaves you with lemons?"

"We make lemonade!" they both exclaim and give each other a high-five as they go to the kitchen to have a top up.

They resume their conversation when Janet returns. "Life has a way of testing your convictions and resolve," Avril continued.

Italy

Some time ago, I had a call from one of our directors asking if I was open to going to Rome to undertake a project with one of the clients. I had done a short-term project that required me to spend time in Rome before, however for this one, I would effectively need to live there and return to London on the weekends. This project was going to span over 2 years. I delightfully consented. This move on the chess board of my career was a quantum leap.

Off course I grabbed it. Adiel was in the last years of secondary school and much older, so being away so much was not going to really affect him as much as it would have, had he being much younger. My amazing mum, yet again stepped up and became the primary caregiver for Adiel in my absence. I made a pact with Adiel that I'd be home every Friday as I did when work took me away from home in his early years.

Every Friday night was family night. So no matter where I am in the world, I will get home so we can play board games, watch movies, or just hang out over some take away food. This worked until Adiel started hanging out with his friends on Fridays.

Once the logistics for my transfer to Rome was completed, I left London with the rest of the team and started my 2-year assignment in Rome. The city stole my heart. Beautiful, full of history, steeped in tradition, it became my favourite city— easily. I absolutely love how much walking one has to do. The enchantment of the availability of designer clothes and shoes in a heartbeat. We lived and worked in a town called Frascati, 20 mins by train outside of Rome. Quaint little place with very hospitable people. It was shocking to find that not very many people speak English, however, we were made very much at home and settled in quite easily. We worked with a fantastic team of people, and it helped that people in the office could speak English communicably.

Living away from England helped cement the resolve I left my therapy with. I had some stability in my emotions and somewhat "found myself". I forged new friendships, assimilated into the Italian culture as best I could and determined to make the experience in that season of my life memorable for all the right reasons. The time I spent in Italy really broaden my perspective and gave me some insight into myself. I know something had shifted in my psyche and I was determined to live my best life, be true to myself and be in touch with my faith convictions, femininity and humanity unapologetically and authentically.

For the first time, I began to explore myself as a black woman because in Italy, I encountered people who were curious and genuinely interested in me as a black woman. I found myself in a sea of white folk, just as I had done in the UK countless times. Only in Italy, I was a tad more conscious. I did not see any black leaders in their field nor did I see role models. There, I was giving value for money and having to navigate that cultural minefield to maximise my productivity, taught me the best version of myself I could be is the authentic Avril. Catholicism is the practised faith. So I had to learn how to practically showcase my faith in a way that will convey the love of God to people who did not necessarily understand or appreciate Christianity in the way I practised it.

I realised how my cultural biases have influenced my decisions, how my religious convictions had made it difficult for me to honestly deal with my personal failures and how societal stereotypes had placed a limitation on my ability to be truly free. I went through a metamorphosis in Italy. I had several growth spurts. I did not have a regular church to attend, yet my commitment to God and my intimacy with Him increased. I read more of and studied the Bible intensely and allowed it to define my way of life—practically.

I understood the love of God in a deeper more meaningful way. I had the time and opportunity to explore the good, the bad and the ugly of culture. I sieved it and to form my own paradigms. So much made sense and to get to a place in life where one's value is not dependent on the opinion of others, the pressures of society, the judgement of the interpretation of their religious convictions or expectations of culture is most liberating. That level of fearlessness and surrender is like fresh ocean breeze on a hot day. Sadly not many people get to that place.

One day after having worked there for about a year, I had a call from an associate from Deloitte (another consulting firm) who was coming to Rome to do some work and asked if we would meet.

I expectantly awaited his arrival and I remember the day he walked into the lobby of the hotel like it was last week. Tall, dark, handsome guy who seemed physically perfect. I felt that familiar tug. The one I felt when I met Leo and Rick. Come on Avril! We've grown now so slow down and let nature take its course, I whispered to myself as I tried to pacify the tingling sensations. *"Hey, I am Chidi"*, he reached out his hand to shake mine with the most charming smile I had seen in a long time. *"Pleasure to meet you, I was expecting you. Hope I make your stay in Rome a delight."* I was calm and composed, although like a duck paddling like crazy underwater, it took every ounce of strength I had to keep my composure.

I got him settled into his room and scheduled a meeting for the following day. That night I had a dream that I was in a strange place, and I heard the knock on the door, when I opened it, I saw him standing there. He said something to me I could not recollect on waking up, but he made me cry. I woke up very perturbed. I called my bestie Emma and explained to her. We talked endlessly, and she warned me to be careful.

The next day I met Chidi as planned, and after our meeting, he asked if he could take me out for a meal one evening that week. Of course I consented. We arranged to meet at the end of the week on Friday.

I phoned Emma excitedly to share this new development. I was cautiously optimistic because this guy was fine, charming and seemed very cultured. I decided I needed to go shopping and get a really nice dinner dress as is typical of women, I did not think I had anything appropriate to wear. Emma was with me on video call as I shopped and we settle on a beautiful black little dress.

On the Friday we were scheduled to meet, I walked out to the lobby where I met Chidi, looking a thousand dollars. He had shaved and smelled like he was bathing in cologne. He made such an effort, and I can't deny he was moving my happiness-o-meter to the right. I felt very comfortable and safe with him. It was clear that the attraction was mutual.

We locked hands as we took a short walk across the

town on the cobbled stone streets. The wall of formality was quickly demolished as we talked and laughed all the way to the restaurant. He put his large arms around my shoulders, and I felt safe, protected, and secure. He was the perfect gentleman—opening the door for me at the restaurant, pulled my chair, and just made sure I was okay all night long. We chatted effortlessly.

I learnt he was widowed. He was a consultant like myself, so we were able to share a lot from the world of work. What did get my heart to move a notch was learning he was a Bible believing Christian and could sing!—a worship leader. I have an insatiable love for music and play the guitar so that was exceptionally exciting.

The Italians I worked with were gracious enough to help us explore and visit other areas in Italy. So each weekend we will take trips in groups. The next weekend we had planned a trip to Venice. I told Chidi and asked him if he would like to join my workmates and I. He was elated and jumped on the idea. I gave him the hotel and rail ticket booking link and he made his bookings. The next seven days were intense we spent endless hours talking and laughing. I felt the reigns of my heart slipping away only this time I was conscious that I knew I was not going to fall hook, line and sinker in love.

The day arrived when we had to leave for Venice. We were all so excited. I was particularly excited that I was sharing this opportunity with someone who I fancied, and I had started enjoying spending time with. My workmates had spoken quite highly of Venice, and I couldn't wait to be there. When we got to Termini, the central train station in Rome where we took the three hour train to Venice, Chidi and I went to the ticket office and requested we travel in a different carriage from the rest of the team so we can have time alone. We bought some food and set off. Chidi made me laugh all the way while playing footsie with me intermittently throughout the journey. We shared work, faith, travel experiences etc.

When we got off the train at Venice, I was so overwhelmed with the beauty of the place that I burst into tears. It was breath taking. Absolutely beautiful. My workmates thought something was wrong that I was that emotional and I just blurted out "I am just so happy to have had an opportunity to be here."

We had a short walk from the train station to the hotel and checked in. We freshened up and met up for dinner, which was delightful. What I found interesting about Italy is that each region may cook the same dish, but it tastes slightly differently. I love the food in Venice. We retired to bed. Late in the night I had a knock on my door, and I pretended to be asleep. I knew it was Chidi. What baffled me was at no point during this trip, in fact, at no point since we met, did he express feelings for me, nor that he desired for us to be a couple. We had flirted but here this Christian man was attempting to have casual sex with me.

The next morning, he met up with me as I headed for breakfast . . . he then put his arms around me and attempted to kiss me. I moved my face and let his kiss land on my cheek. I then put my hand on his chest and said "My darling. I know we are in one of, if not the most romantic places ever, however, I am sorry, I don't play emotional gymnastics. We met, clicked and are getting on very well. I have no clarity from you in terms of what you feel or where this is going. Indulging in any form of emotional entanglement at this point will complicate issues. Please let's enjoy Venice as a place and let's continue to bond and let things take a natural evolution".

He seemed somewhat embarrassed, but I noticed flames of anger in his eyes and certainly he was enraged. He pulled away from me and muttered something under his breath which I did not get clear but sounded like 'what a bloody waste of my time.' I asked him to repeat himself but of course he refused to.

All off a sudden this cute and handsome man who was so charming, turned into an evil beast. He walked off ahead into me to the breakfast hall. I joined him after getting some food. He was suddenly cold and indifferent. My other workmates, pretty much left us to ourselves. We had drawn up a list of places we can see and things we can do in Venice and I asked Chidi what he fancied doing. Without looking at the tourist guide, he simply said "whatever floats your boat". Chidi was being awkward, and it was making me very uncomfortable. The rest of the trip turned out to be a living hell.

He looked around yawned and said loudly, "my, my,, my, I can't wait to bring my girlfriend here. It has always been a dream of mine to propose to my future wife on a gondola". I pretended not to hear. He sluggishly walked behind me and was being deliberately obnoxious. He was disinterested in every suggestion I made. However, he used the time to tell me I was short and how frankly he is not interested in short girls. He told me my eyes were big and basically looking at me closely, he realised how ugly and unattractive I really am.

In fact, he was disinterested in any woman past the age of 30 as he was looking for a wife and wanted babies with a woman who had fresh young eggs. After a few hours of insults, I suggested that maybe it's best if we decide to do different things as to me it was clear he no longer enjoyed my company. He words were like knives being thrust in me and he seemed to take much pleasure in taking a real dig at me. I kept quiet for the most part and withdrew myself from him.

I couldn't believe how horrible the whole trip turned out. I had to stomach sitting with him on the train all the way back to Rome the next day. He looked at me and said "I am surprised that you thought you could be my significant other. I love in Canada, you live in the UK. I will have slept with you and left you." I was thankful for the lucky escape I had had from this wolf in sheep's clothing. When I remember how loving and charming he was when we met, I could hardly believe who I was dealing with.

When we got back, he decided to check out of the hotel and moved to another hotel across town. I went to my room and the impact of the words he said really hurt my feelings. I called Emma and cried my eyes out! I was so thankful I did not give myself away cheaply. The Monday after our trip was a public holiday so we returned to work on Tuesday. Most of that Monday, I was in deep thought and thankfully I was able to think very rationally about the whole weekend and put a lot in perspective. Clearly I was in a much stronger place and unlike my former encounters, I realised his lack of character was his problem, not mine.

On Tuesday, I woke up really early and I felt I needed to bring a proper closure to whatever friendship I had was developing with Chidi. By this time he had called me a thousand times and I did not answer because I felt I needed the time to process everything. It was clear to me that he deliberately went out of his way to hurt me the way he felt hurt at me stopping his advances in its tracks. I needed to use this opportunity to provide him room to grow and I wanted to protect other women who he would meet in the future so I decided to write him the following:

Good morning Chidi,

I woke up this morning and as I listened to a Yolanda Adams track, I reminisced on out time especially the time we spent in Venice. You may not have realised but I am extremely sensitive and this weekend left me a little bruised. I had to wait this long to write or say what I had to say because I really needed to establish that I was not dealing with you from a place of malice or revenge or any other negative emotion associated with how I was feeling.

I decided to have a pep talk with myself to address how I am feeling and how I we go on from here. Here were my thoughts:

Avril, Learn! Analyse your friends and analyse with even more scrutiny those who you dare to love. In friendship constantly ask who adds, subtracts, multiplies and divide. You will know who to upgrade, downgrade or totally terminate.

Not everyone deserves a front seat in the movie of your life. Anyone not adding value should take a back seat. Those who feel you have want they want but can't afford you will seek to minimise your worth and marginalise your existence. They will make you feel small, under-valued, insecure, and belittle your worth. Those who see no greatness in their own lives and consider their goals unattainable will seek to thwart yours and try to see nothing good in your own life.

Never treat someone as a priority when he or she only sees you like an option. Never put temporary people in permanent positions. Be bold, make decisions and position yourself for victory. Lions don't mingle with cats. Not everyone can carry the weight of who you are. Never go on a journey with someone going in another direction or nowhere at all. When you sense the end of a season, make a shift or you will be held back and frustrated. Be celebrated not tolerated.

My dear, I have asked God to bless me beyond my capacity to receive. His Word promises to open the heavens and pour out a blessing more than I can contain. My cup will run over. Even if God does no more, so far He has blown my mind, BUT, He has promise to continue his work in me and so my prayer is that He will give me the wisdom to enlarge my capacity to receive more as He opens the floodgates. I will be blessed with more than enough and as my cup runs over, I will be a blessing to many!

God is going to take me to heights that are inconceivable by many. That climb is going to require that I lighten my load. Our friendship has caused me some pain and not served the purpose I thought and I feel I must pull back.

I wonder if you ever stopped to replay the weekend in your mind and thought why I was so excited to go on a trip with you and so sad when we did? When I was alone with my thoughts, I realised your being with me, your words and insinuations had left me feeling, ugly, undesirable and insecure. I am hurt because for the first time in a long time, I realised the enemy had taken a stab at my achieved wholeness.

Ha, ha, ha. I am not ignorant of the devil's devices!!! The devil's work is to steal, kill and destroy but I Avril will NOT be his prey! He has done enough, but this time I see him attempting to work through you. He will not steal my joy, he will not kill my dreams and he will not destroy my life!

I will arise as the champion for the wholeness that God has given me and I will go from nation to nation teaching the things I have learnt. I will let women everywhere know who to decipher agent of destruction to their self-worth and how to stay well clear of them.

The fight is fixed and at the end of the day I win, God has told me numerous times that I must be still and know that He is God. As long as I stay in the steps He has ordered, whether I am mad or glad, depressed or Joyful, in this life, I just have to be still and let God fight for me!

I will definitely go back to Venice with my true love. That's for sure. I will re-write my history there and make it a pleasant and memorable location.

You really made me feel like I was robbing you of an experience you did not want to share with me. It was bizarre. You kept talking about your future wife the whole time. Okay, you want to go and propose on a gondola.

Why did you, knowing that is what you dreamt, jump on a train with a woman who you know you don't want to make your wife, go to a place that was so special to you and decide to make it hard for her after making a failed pass at her.

Ok before you came, I naively, thought we could platonically hang out, travel together and be friends. I am leaving you alone!

Since I met you, I have asked myself a number of questions. What does this friendship do for me? Who am I in your life? How much value am I adding to you? This weekend with you helped me put so much in perspective. I know you much more than you think I do. The first few months of any relationship I have whether it is a youth I am mentoring, development of working relations on a new job or a personal friendship, I am in an observant mode so that I can win and that relationship can survive and flourish.

Somehow I perceive unfortunately we exist in parallel universes and I am not sure our worlds will ever meet. Even though I felt there was so much we had in common, we both seemingly want different things out of life and indeed out of each other.

I am going to step aside so I can give you the opportunity to forge the friendships you desire. I do not intend to be like the other "friends" you have. You have asked me to cover you in prayer so I will do that as much as I can, I think you have so many women throwing themselves at you that you don't stop to <u>sensitively</u> handle people who may genuinely care for you and relationships that could become pillars in your life.

In the time we were together for e.g. not once could I recollect you paid me a single compliment. It's almost like you thought I liked you and you needed to make a point that it was not mutual. Ha, ha, ha. I am not ignorant of the devil's devices.

I thought at least we liked each other (note I did not say love . . . like as in fond of, enjoyed each other's company etc.), but somehow you almost seemed to be repelled by me after you tried making a pass on me that failed. Your whole body language changed.

Even when we returned to Frascati and you opted to check out of the hotel. It was almost like the magic of the delight I felt when you were around me vanished into thin air. You were with me but no longer with me.

Somehow I feel things have changed in a strange way even before our friendship could blossom.

In the years I have walked with God, the greatest lesson I have learnt is that I must trust God blindly.

I cannot let your opinion, convictions and desires be my obligation. I have concluded that in my life, I do not need the accessories of being popular. I just need the faith that comes with being chosen. I know that every desire of my heart will materialise. Whether it be marriage, my streams of income opportunities or that of being a mother again.

It may not and definitely has not happened in the time and way I thought but, I KNOW it will happen in God's way and God's time!

It may be your style to get close to a girl, maybe even get intimate but try your best to let her wipe off the idea of any long term commitment from you by undermining her looks or declaring your desires which are completely contrary to who she is. I remember with distaste your reluctance to get into a gondola with me and my disappointment in finding out that it is because you wanted to share that moment ideally with your future wife. At that moment I completely regret ever going to Venice with you.

A thousand and one things were going through my mind but I never speak in the heat of a moment. I need to process things, analyse, make sense objectively, learn my lessons and then communicate. That way I risk not hurting people back.

I feel it is important to write you because (1) My thoughts are clearer. (2) I feel that if I was hurt I shouldn't pretend not to have been so at least I can learn from it (which I have) and hopefully in communicating with you, you will understand where I am coming from and learn something too for your future dealings with others.

There are much better ways of handling a girl. In fact

let me help you as you seem to lack basic respect for women. My experience with you is that you don't fully understand emotional implications in dealing with a woman.

If you know there is no chance in Hell you will ever be with someone in a relationship, have boundaries—that's integrity.

Even if she offers you her bed, take the high ground and refuse. I know as a guy from time to time you might want to engage in casual sex to "take the edge off" but I came into your life on a different premise and frankly I don't know how you handle that from a Christian perspective as you mentioned you are a practising Christian.

You are a nice guy, you are good looking, tall, single, and have a lot going for you. I can understand if girls gravitate to you like bees to honey. So while it might stroke your ego to tease out emotions from women, remember that the seeds we sow come back to us many times over so be careful.

It is clear I am not your cup of tea and boy did you make a point! I may be too old (in your eyes) to be the mother of your children or too short and petite to be a life companion, and that's ok.

You have a right to desire who you want but let me tell you a secret. I am beautiful, intelligent, successful, saved, whole, yes short—only 5'4", petite, but spiritually mature, financially independent, emotionally balanced, loving and loved by many!

My husband is going to love me just the way I am. My complexion, my height, my weight, my funny shaped toes, big eyes, my chatty personality, my childlikeness, my attention to detail, my love for people, my kind, sensitive and soft heart, my surgery-scarred body, my love for travelling and my insatiable desire for learning—he is going to love it all! Neither my beauty, nor my success or intelligence will intimidate him. He will celebrate me, nurture my creativity and go down on his knees many times to thank God for making me and bring me into his life.

I will add value to him and he to me. He will speak life to my dreams and I will stand behind him to be the steam he needs to be propelled to the heights of greatness he dreams off. Together we will be a winning team. We will be best friends effortlessly, have children if we desire and we will be each other's sounding board. He will allow me to develop confidence in his ability to care for me and he will be careful about the things he says and how he handles me as a woman. I am sure it might sound as noise to your ears but I need to declare it so that the devil who attempted to use you and his cohorts can hear me loud and clear!

I have made a commitment to myself to be authentic. Sometimes being stripped to the core is the only way to become more. That core is where the most profound expression of yourself, the most authentic you emanates from. I want to be all that God has called me to be and all He expects and has equipped me to do so I must walk and let my life blossom with the associations that validate me, appreciate me and love me in spite of myself. I have tried to live with a consciousness that I am accountable to God. In the dealings with my fellow man, I have to the best of my knowledge and ability never tried to violate another person, either by what I say or do.

In this past weekend, not that I can recall, but, if I said anything that was hurtful I am sorry. I felt we got on well and had great rapport. The way you handled me after you tried kissing me is what was most destructive to our budding friendship and I am sorry that I gave you the room to hurt me like you did. Maybe even insisting that I wanted to do the gondola ride was irritating to—you, I don't know. If in any way I offended you, please accept my apologies.

You are released from the yoke of offence. The irritations of your expressed sentiments and inadvertent harm done with words are now gone. I made sure I dealt with my feelings of hurt because I wanted this letter to be constructive not destructive. I forgive you completely and want you to know I hold nothing against you. I wish you the very best that life offers.

The world is a small place and I am sure our paths may cross again if God wills. If not, I know the seed of greatness lies within you. I pray that whenever I hear of you or from you it will be with reasons to give thanks and praise to God.

I know you will do well. Be strong.

Avril.

In a matter of weeks, my encounter with Chidi was well and truly behind me and I knew unquestionably that something had shifted in how I will allow another human being to treat me especially in the context of a love relationship.

There was a freedom and a fearlessness in my approach to life and that my friends is what gives me the skip in my step and the confidence that effervesces from my being.

Girls, I found myself. I learnt how to love myself and to put my interests first. I decided that before I embark on a pursuit of love, I am going to make Avril happy.

I have travelled all over the place. I love travelling. I realised it has intrigued me to understand what drives human survival within the context of local cultures. I have come to realise that when the chips are down, all humans—whether black, white, Asian or Hispanic, we all have the same basic needs: food, shelter, clothing, love, safety and above all, salvation. I have come to love people at a very deep level.

I love to cook. I have learnt to cook cuisine from the different places across the globe I have travelled and enjoy the food. So when people ask me what is your favourite dish? It very much depends on the desires of my palette that day.

I forged healthy friendships and do things with like-minded people who share similar interests. I love theatre, art, and museums. I love music. I have learnt to dance salsa, and I play the guitar.

I allow my life to be a torch for others who feel they can't make it out.

I love life and I am living it. We are meant to live not just exist and I am determined to enjoy my life, not endure through it.

When will marriage happen for me? I honestly don't know. But what I do know it that when it does, it will be totally worth the wait.

LIFE LESSONS

"Wow Avril, that was a thriller!" Janet exclaimed. "Who would have thought when I left my home today, I would be take on such an amazing journey?" Janet said. "I have experienced such a range of emotions and you know what, every woman can identify. Single, married, divorced, loved up or even desiring to be loved. Oh my goodness, look at the time. Let me call hubby again before he comes looking for me!"

"Avril", Rosa said quite pensively. "Look at me. I have sat here and cried and laughed and felt hope and truly I am honoured to be your friend. Even though I know pockets of your experiences, I am so very deeply touched, so moved and frankly, transformed. Having gone through all you did, what will you say are the key life lessons you learnt and how do they shape how you do the business of life now?"

God is our ever present help!

You know, in the darkest time of my life, I realised that there is no pit so deep that God is not deeper still. There is no place so dark and so remote that God is not able to reach and rescue.

There were so many times in my marriage when the psychological load of embarrassment outweighed my rational thinking to give myself the room and opportunity to live. There were times when I was concerned about what people would say about me not being able to hold my marriage down.

There were times when subconsciously I felt as a Christian it was not okay to be a divorcee because I was supposed to forgive or walk by faith. Culturally, African women are raise to bear pain. African men are openly polygamous and it is expected that the wife should turn a blind eye until the husband decides to focus and prioritise their marriage. To add insult to injury, not a single member of my family was divorced. So the thought of going through a divorce not even being 30yrs of age, was overwhelming. Black women are raised to be strong. To keep it together. Interestingly, there is a stigma that every divorcee knows only too well—"it must be your fault".

When I got separated from Akpon, I was not only in a low place emotionally, I was homeless and in debt. All my earthly possessions were in 3 black bags. Even though I had furnished the flat we lived in I could take nothing out as I had short notice and nowhere to go. I was a mental mess.

One day as I have aforementioned, I took my focus off my personal pain and put it on Jesus. I came to a place where I learnt what it meant to "cast your cares and burdens on Him". There is such power in total surrender to God. I got to that place when I worshipped for 6 hours straight. I was not going to move from that place until God came on the scene. I purposed that if God is real and truly He cares, I needed the darkness I dwelt in to shift and He did! God stepped in and pulled me out of the pit I was in. He showered me with His love and gave me a reason to live. I remember that encounter as if it was yesterday. So powerfully transforming. Now over 15 years from that experience, I have never got to a place that low mentally or emotionally.

On a practical level, He showed me a way out. There is a passage of scripture from the Bible I read as I was evolving that I'd love to share with you.

Elijah and the Widow at Zarephath— 1 Kings 17: 7—16

7 Sometime later the brook dried up because there had been no rain in the land. 8 Then the word of the Lord came to him: 9 "Go at once to Zarephath (A) in the region of Sidon and stay there. I have directed a widow (B) there to supply you with food." 10 So he went to Zarephath. When he came to the town gate, a widow was there gathering sticks. He called to her and asked, "Would you bring me a little water in a jar so I may have a drink?"(C) 11 As she was going to get it, he called, "And bring me, please, a piece of bread."

12 "As surely as the Lord your God lives," she replied, "I don't have any bread—only a handful of flour in a jar and a little olive oil (D) in a jug. I am gathering a few sticks to take home and make a meal for myself and my son, that we may eat it—and die."

13 Elijah said to her, "Don't be afraid. Go home and do as you have said. But first make a small loaf of bread for me from what you have and bring it to me, and then make something for yourself and your son. 14 For this is what the Lord, the God of Israel, says: 'The jar of flour will not be used up and the jug of oil will not run dry until the day the Lord sends rain (E) on the land.'"

15 She went away and did as Elijah had told her. So there was food every day for Elijah and for the woman and her family. 16 For the jar of flour was not used up and the jug of oil did not run dry, in keeping with the word of the Lord spoken by Elijah.

When I stumbled on this scripture, I realised that so many times when we feel we are at our lowest and there is no way out God always has a plan. All we need is to open ourselves to be guided and be courageous enough to be obedient to follow His leading. Sometimes it may seem crazy, unrealistic and abstract, but God knows best.

When I cried out to God to change my story, I was effectively homeless, my Master's degree incomplete, without a plan or money to go back, in debt and a really bad place. As the days went by, I felt better emotionally, my thoughts became clearer. I felt I desired to have my own place so I sought the services of an estates agent. Through a series of God—ordained meetings, I met the financial adviser who helped me with the clearing of my debt and purchasing of my first home. God ALWAYS has us.

I also decided to return to University to complete me degree. Which I successfully finished with distinction. God sent the broker like an angel to help me. Even at University, I joined a study group that took turns in babysitting so I could have breaks to focus on my studies. God gave me my own jar of oil and made ways when there seemed none. Now I know unequivocally, experientially, that with God, I am a majority and nothing, absolutely nothing is impossible for Him to achieve through me.

You are who God says you are:

I realised it is so easy to have your humanity undermined and your self-worth sabotaged. For the most part, I had a happy and secure childhood but a few traumatic incidents had had an impact on me in ways I had no idea about. The devil capitalised on that and desired to mess me up.

Even though I am considered rather beautiful; growing up that was not affirmed by my mother and I never felt worthy of love. Entering into adulthood, the programming instilled in me that the choice of a partner should be limited to the church that limited my partner selection greatly. Eventually I was reeled into a snare an ended up marrying my husband. From his own brokenness, he carried on the devil's work of rubber stamping the notion that I was unlovable, I was left betrayed and somewhat broken, hurt and wrecked by the abandonment and rejection I face at his hands.

I was left feeling inadequate as a woman, incapable, unworthy, uncertain and in a place of pain that seemed to ooze from the wounds that never seemed to heal. On the outside everything looked on point. I had a lovely home. My son was attending a top private school. As a small family unit we went on holidays twice a year. I had gotten rid of a useless husband but inside there was an emotional voids and total confusion about this thing called love.

As a young girl, I had my appendix removed at 14, in my early 20's I had 2 lumpectomies, having my child I had a caesarean, furthermore I have had 3 polypectomies and a myomectomy. I carry surgical scars all over my body. I have a well-toned athletic body yet I was sensitive about surgical scars and in a sense it affected my view of myself.

When I went into therapy and learnt everyone has a story and I had to learn to love and respect myself for others to do the same. We are not meant to be perfect, we are meant to be whole. In my journey to wholeness, As a practising Christian, I started to reprogram my subconscious to see myself the way God sees me from how the Bible describes me and what being in relationship with God gives me access to.

When the penny dropped in my subconscious, restoration took place in my life. I realised consciously I had a better barometer of measurement of my worth. I t was no longer dependent on who likes me or not but all that mattered was the knowledge that God has me and with Him I was a winner in all things.

"How did you reprogram your subconscious?" Janet asked inquisitively. "You remember I said earlier about my I AM's? I recited them every day for over a year and I still do even today." Let me share:

"Take these scriptures and read them to yourself and trust me, change and enhancement will come to you, no matter, where you are in your life. You don't have to be downtrodden. Better still if you are. But in whatever place you are on your journey, let the Word of God define your identity."

Romans 8:16:	I am a child of God
Psalm 107:2	I am redeemed from the hand of the enemy
Colossians 1:13-14	I am forgiven
Ephesians 2:8	I am saved by grace through faith
Romans 5:1	I am justified
1 Corinthians 1:30	I am sanctified
2 Corinthians 5:17	I am a new creature, old things have passed away
2 Peter 1:4	I am a partaker of God's divine nature
Galatians 3:13	I am redeemed from the curse of the law
Colossians 1:13	I am delivered from the powers of darkness
Romans 8:14	I am led by the Spirit of God
Psalm 91:11	I am kept in safety wherever I go
Philippians 4:19	I have all my needs met by Christ Jesus
1 Peter 5:7	I cast all my cares on Jesus
Ephesians 6:10	I am strong in the Lord and in the power of His might.
Romans 8:17	I am an heir of God and a joint heir with Christ.
Galatians 3:13-14	I am an heir to the blessings of Abraham
2 Corinthians 5:7	I am walking by faith and not by sight

2 Corinthians 10:4	I am casting down vain imaginations
2 Corinthians 10:5	I am bring every thought captive to the obedience of Christ.
Romans 12: 1-2	I am being transformed by the renewing of my mind
1 Corinthians 3:9	I am a labourer together with God
2 Corinthians 5:21	I am the righteousness of God in Christ.
Ephesians 5:1	I am an imitator of Christ.
Matthew 5:14	I am the light of the world
Psalm 34:1	I am blessing the Lord at all times and continually praising the Lord with my mouth.
John 1:12	I am a child of God
Romans 5:1	I have peace with God
1 Corinthians 3:16	I am a temple of the Holy Spirit.
James 1:5	I have access to God's wisdom.
Hebrews 4:16	I am helped by God
Romans 5:11	I am reconciled by God
Romans 8:1	I am not condemned by God
Romans 5:19	I have Christ's righteousness
2 Corinthians 5:20	I am Christ's ambassador
Jeremiah 31:3	I am tenderly loved by God
2 Corinthians 2:15	I am the sweet fragrance of Christ to God

Colossian 1:22	I am blameless and beyond reproach
Matthew 5:13	I am the salt of the Earth
John 15:1	I am a branch on Christ's vine
John 15:5	I am Christ's friend
John 15:6	I am chosen by Christ to bear fruit
I Corinthians 6:17	I am united to the Lord, one spirit with Him
1 Corinthians 12:27	I am a member of Christ's body
Ephesians 1:1	I am a saint
Colossians 3:3	I am hidden with Christ in God.
Colossians 3:12	I am chosen by God, holy and dearly loved
1 Thessalonians 5:5	I am a child of the light
Hebrews 3:1	I am holy and share in God's heavenly calling
Hebrews 2:11	I am sanctified
1 Peter 2:5	I am one of God's living stones, being built up in Christ as a spiritual house.
1 Peter 2:9-10	I am a member of a chosen race, a royal priesthood, a holy nation and people belonging to God.
Colossians 2:7	I am firmly rooted and built up in Christ
1 John 5:18	I am born of God and the evil one cannot touch me.
I Corinthians 2:16	I have the mind of Christ

Ephesians 3:12	I may approach God with boldness freedom and confidence
Colossians 1:13	I have been rescued from Satan's domain and transferred into the kingdom of light.
Colossians 2:10	I have been made complete in Christ
2 Timothy 1:7	I have been given a spirit of power, love and a sound mind
2 Peter 1:4	I have been given great and precious promises by God
John 1:12	I am a princess in God's kingdom
1 Corinthians 6:19	I have been bought with a price and I belong to God
Ephesians 1:5	I have been adopted as God's child
Ephesians 2:18	I have direct access to God through the Holy Spirit
Romans 8:28	I am sure that all things are working together for my good.
Romans 8:31	I am free from all condemnation
Romans 8:35	I cannot be separated from the love of God.
2 Corinthians 1:21	I have been established, anointed and sealed by God
Philippians 1:6	I am confident that the good work that God began in me will be perfected
Philippians 3:20	I am a citizen of heaven

Acts 1:8	I am a personal witness of Christ
Ephesians 2:6	I am seated with Christ in heavenly places
Ephesians 2:10	I am God's workmanship
Philippians 4:13	I can do all things through Christ who strengthens me

These scriptures are straight out of the Bible. I do not just read them but I pray with them with knowledge and assurance. As I declared these things to myself, they became my reality. We frame our world by the power of our words and here I am today, a true testament of the fact that you have what you say—healed and whole.

Forgiveness is the greatest gift of freedom we have

I have a few guys that are very dear to my heart. One of them is a guy who I knew before I was even married. He became like a brother to me, a confidant and a true friend. Out of share boredom, we used to gate crash parties together religiously over a period of time. We had a lot of fun. He subsequently got married and had 3 beautiful children. One day he asked me to cook him an African dish which he really likes. I did, froze it and told him he could come by and collect it when he found it convenient.

One Saturday morning, he called to let me know he would be picking up the food, even joking that he hoped I had not squandered it. He did come by but I was in the shower. I asked my mum to look in the freezer but she couldn't find the bowl so I came out of the shower dried myself and went downstairs in my towel.

My mum walked away when I turned up and I was left in the kitchen with my friend. As soon as I bent over to find the food in the freezer he pulled off my towel. I was shocked and wondered why he would do such a thing. I turned and looked at him and he grinned and said "nice view from where I am standing". He thought it was funny, however I was deeply offended. I felt violated, hurt and betrayed. He figured that by the way I look at him. I handed him his food and ushered him to the door.

Why do men like taking chances, I thought. Why do something that can potentially damage years of a good friendship? I could not shift the feeling of betrayal and offence. The next week I was invited to a cook out at one of my cousins' house. This group of people were my close family and we had hung out several times before. Traditionally we turn up at each other's houses share food, board games, dancing competitions etc.

I arrived well before the others. I asked the host what she had for us to eat to which she responded "grilled chicken wings". I asked "is that all? Do you have plum tomatoes? Let me rustle up some Jollof rice quickly". She said she needed to make a quick dash to the store to get some but it was fine because it was only 5 mins down the road.

As soon as she left, another one of my cousins arrived. I explained our host had gone to the shop as I suggested it will be nice to have some Jollof to go with the chicken and I will be happy to cook it. My cousin started ranting and ripping into me. She insulted me no end calling me all sorts of unprintable things. I was horrified. The others arrived and before the host returned she went out, explained to them and they joined in the berating of my character.

I spent the whole evening wondering what I had done to deserve the verbal crucifixion I received. The one who started insulting me was a cousin I had taken under my wing as a baby sister. I drove home that evening in a flood of tears.

So many times before, while I had the legal wrangling with Akpon to get custody of Adiel, I remember several times, just seeing him triggered so many emotions. From rage to disgust to nausea. I had such a deep seated anger and unforgiveness toward him. There were times when I will get into my car and drive around hoping I will see him and knock him over. I could not reconcile how a man can walk into a virgin's life, take advantage of her vulnerability, abuse her, leave her with a child he doesn't raise, cause so much damage to her emotionally, psychologically and leave her financially broke, yet be free in their conscience to go on and live their life.

My notion was if I am hurt, he should be hurt too. There were so many times I thought I had forgiven him, yet something would happen after that decision that will open every wound I have ever been inflicted with and it was a vicious cycle that hindered my ability to forgive and bury the pain.

The incident with my cousins was on a Friday. I woke up on Saturday morning and my brother picked up Adiel to go spend some time with him. When they left the heaviness and sadness and hurt was still in my heart. I walked to the living room and with tears streaming down my eyes, as I reminisced on the night before laid on the floor and prayed.

"Father God, what life lesson are you trying to teach me?

Last week I was betrayed by my friend, this week everyone ganged up on me and completely slated me unfairly. I am finding this so painful because the one who led them Lord, you know I love her like my own sister. I have been such a blessing to her in the past. Now I am wondering why this is happening to me." All off a sudden, I felt the presence of the Lord with me. I knew God heard the cry of my heart. I was in a place of brokenness before him. The Bible says God will not despise a broken and a contrite heart.

As I dialogued with God, I had another encounter that taught me a very powerful life lesson. The Lord began to speak to my heart. He showed me that I was carrying a lot of bitterness and unforgiveness. "I forgave them Lord". I protested. "When you came to me and asked for forgiveness for sin, do I forgive you"? "Yes Lord" I answered. "You know how I do it? I take your sins and throw them in the sea of forgetfulness. I remember them no more. When you truly forgive, you let it go. You deal with the person like the issue never happened. I have admonished you to forgive as I have forgiven you. In fact my word say 70 times 7. You are holding on to too much pain and its destroying you". All of a sudden I went into what I can only describe as a trance.

I saw myself back in the corridors of time and saw a replay of encounters I had had in which I was offended. Incidents that were so far back that it had to take God for me to recollect. I saw myself in primary school, in secondary school, with my childhood and teenage friends. I felt the offences afresh, each time an incident would be replayed to me, I called out the name and names of the people that had offended me and released forgiveness toward them.

This encounter took me all the way to my marriage right

unto what happened the night before. I came to myself and I was still on the floor only I felt 1 million percent lighter. I felt a physical weight was lifted off of me. I knew without a shadow of doubt, I was free from the bondage of unforgiveness.

The Christmas festivities went on and before the year rolled over, I had a call from the Church radio station that there was a popular programme that they wanted me to be featured on. The producer, found my story inspiring wanted me to share 'tips for overcoming adversity'. I was dumbfounded that someone found my story inspirational. Anyway, I went to the station and shared my story on radio it was a short one hour show that made provision for people to call in.

I was amazed that the programme was very widely aired with listeners tuning in from the Caribbean and the United States. Interestingly, the biggest message I had for the listeners was that they needed to come to a place when they truly, completely and totally forgive their offenders. It empowers you to soar higher. It liberates you to get to a better place. Forgiving someone has nothing to do with them apologising. One needs to get to a place where they choose mercy over judgement. The interesting thing is that as you show mercy to others, God shows mercy to you and great things begin to happen in your life.

The radio show was a major success. So many people were touched and in one way or the other, my story resonated with them. A few weeks later, a friend of mine's mum passed away. I went to the funeral and lo and behold, after several years, I bumped into Akpon. To my amazement. The sickening feeling and the rage, hurt, disgust, bitterness and anger was gone. Sometimes seeing him after we were separated, I will shiver, my body had physical spasms spun out of utter disgust. For the first time since I knew him, even before we got married, I pitied him. I remembered the stories he told me when we were dating about him and his brother being abandoned by their father.

I remembered the broken relationship he had with his mother. Now I saw someone who to be had let the devil use him to attempt to destroy my life and hurt his own child. I felt sorry for him and the love of God toward him. I saw a man who need truly experience God's grace and forgiveness. He couldn't look at me. He walked past me a few times, pretending not to know me. I then walked up to him and said hello. He was confused and embarrassed. He couldn't even respond properly.

I was amazed at myself and of a truth, in that moment, angels in heaven and demons in Hell bore witness that finally, the yoke of unforgiveness was broken. I had a chit chat with him. Before walking away, I said in jest "I hope you have not forgotten you have a son". I opened my phone and showed him a picture of Adiel. He looked at him briefly and turned away, seemingly overwhelmed with guilt. He hastened to walk away from me and muttered almost inaudibly "I hope he is doing well". I did not have time to respond. He was gone in a flash.

Someone once said, holding on to offence, hurt and pain and refusing to forgive, is like drinking poison and waiting for the offender to die. I came into a truth that has influenced many other encounters I have had in life since then. I have come into a place of great liberty. Forgiveness is probably the biggest life lesson I learnt.

Hope! Never a full stop where God put a comma.

After I settled in life and came into a place of emotional wholeness, I allowed my life to be a fountain of blessing. I have done well career wise and enjoy getting out of bed every day and giving value for money on my job. I serve the next generation by helping young people avoid the pitfalls of making the wrong decisions in choosing a mate. I have learnt a few life lessons and I am thankful for my journey. It has been worth it all.

I went on to adopt several orphanages and travel widely giving those disadvantaged children hope, mothering and an assurance of God's love for them. I feel truly blessed, some of those children will grow up to remember me as 'that woman from London' and may never be able to repay me, but what a joy it is to be a blessing.

When you learn, teach! When you are blessed, give! That is what gives our story purpose. That is how one becomes fruitful and multiply. I often say not even the sky is the limit, it is just a stepping stone to the next level.

As my financial adviser said in admonishing me not to continue the cycle of self-destruction, in this life, if someone takes your stove. Never, ever let them take your fire—ever! That is the very essence of who you are. As we let our fire blaze, we light up the pathways for others and as we shine, even in a dark place, we become the hands, heart and voice of God extended to humanity. The beauty of walking up to Akpon without an iota of bitterness, was one of the most powerful moments in our existence.

Every now and again as sojourners on this side of eternity we may need a little help on this race called life. Disappointments, delays, disillusionment, divorce, discouragement, debt, death, disease, debilitations are all distractions from our destiny.

Be diligent in protecting every part of you. Life will throw you many challenges that will threaten to change your character. You will learn you cannot be patterned after another human's opinion off or desire for you, and that the authentic you has no pattern. Quiet the doubts, mute the fears and drown the voice that will convince you to betray your worth. As you find your true self, you will learn validation. Never let someone else validate you at the expense of your dignity.

When you realise that only God can define you, that you are awesome, that you are on a winning streak and when the realisation hits home, that He God who made you, had declared even before you were born that you will always triumph, you will live and go through life with unimaginable peace.

You are worthy of the best, no matter how many times you have been broken. I remember an illustration I once saw. Someone took a £20 note nice and crisp. He held it up and said how much is this. Everyone to his hearing said £20. He crumbled it spoke to the note harshly, placed on the ground and stamped on it. Cussed it out and said "I don't even like the machine that printed you, now I bet you stink, I have walked all over you". Then he picked up the note, crumpled and dirty. Then he asked again "how much is this" everyone said "£20". He then said if I took it to a store how much will it be worth? He heard back a resounding "£20". He then said "no matter what you go through, don't ever let that diminish your worth".

The true test of strength is not in the breaking, it is in your determination to recover. Not giving up on God means you are trusting Him and accepting that you are deserving of His love, grace and favour in spite of your mistakes. You are never out of His reach

If you are still hoping after you have been broken you're stronger than you believe. Make a decision not to allow what hurt you to change you into someone you are not. If you want to know what it feels like to be lucky that you are still alive, take a deep breath—that's it! You're alive!!! Where there is life, there is hope! You are alive! Now, live!!!

No woman should die in a storm. Let the winds take you higher. We are more powerful than we know. Victory belongs to those who, in spite of their fears push through every battle and enforce the victories we already have.

Printed in Great Britain
by Amazon